T0208904

The Bodyguard Blueprint

A Field Guide to Executive Protection Business Success

by
Lenny Bogdanos

authorHOUSE®

AuthorHouse™
1663 Liberty Drive
Bloomington, IN 47403
www.authorhouse.com
Phone: 1 (800) 839-8640

Published by AuthorHouse 06/28/2019

ISBN: 978-1-7283-0877-7 (sc)
ISBN: 978-1-7283-0875-3 (hc)
ISBN: 978-1-7283-0876-0 (e)

Library of Congress Control Number: 2019904485

Print information available on the last page.

This book is printed on acid-free paper.

Contents

Foreword

I always start out any class or course that I teach by making this same statement: One of my least favorite topics is talking about myself. I believe that success is not only measured by accomplishing things that you believe you need to achieve success, whether it be money, property, a family, or an honorable reputation. There are many different things that people measure success by. I believe that in order to be truly successful, you must achieve those things while maintaining humility. That is the true challenge. A belief that I know is shared by Mr. Lenny Bogdanos. However, to lend credibility to my endorsement of Lenny's latest book, *The Bodyguard Blueprint*, I must share a little of my background.

As a police officer for twenty-four years in two different states and serving for thirteen of those years as a member of a Special Weapons and Tactic team (SWAT) as a team member, leader, and commander, I participated in and led hundreds of missions and countless hours of tactical training as both a student and instructor. It has been an honor to have trained with and instructed with members of law enforcement, private contractors, and specialized military units, including the National Tactical Officer's Association, Federal Law Enforcement Training Center, and in dignitary protection with the Secret Service.

In 1991, prior to my career in law enforcement, I met Lenny Bogdanos when we both worked as lifeguards at the Long Recreation Center in Clearwater, Florida. Lenny was an eighteen-year-old black belt in Tae Kwon Do and trained relentlessly for a shot at the 1992 Olympics. In the end he would be offered a position, and team captain, on the U.S. World team and becoming a world champion in 1994. He had an obvious drive to be the very best in whatever he set his mind to. We forged a lifelong friendship and mutual respect that continues to this day.

In 2011, I served on the Tampa Bay Regional Planning Committee to plan the law-enforcement response to the Republican National Convention (RNC). I wanted to bring in an instructor to conduct refresher training in executive protection for the upcoming RNC. As a SWAT responsibility, I believed it would be highly advantageous to offer my team members the opportunity to perform dignitary protection for the numerous VIPs and dignitaries rather than being assigned to do field force riot control. Think of this: somewhere right now, some protestor is urinating and defecating in a bucket in order to save it for a future protest six months or more from now, in order to dump it on a police officer who is stuck doing riot control. As fate would have it, Lenny had recently founded his company *International Executive Protection* and was training executive protection students in preparation for the RNC. Of course, I took Lenny's course and it was beyond fantastic. In his many years as an executive protection officer, advanced training in EP work, and developing training curriculum, Lenny had honed his craft and had a passion for teaching others the correct way of doing things.

On the heels of the successful RNC, Lenny asked me to help him further develop the training portion of his company. Together, we wrote and taught lesson plans for embus and debus (boarding and exiting a vehicle), client movement, and handgun and sub gun firearms. Through working with Lenny on training development and delivery, I watched and learned as Lenny grew his business from a handful of protection specialists to a major security company able to run long-term and complex operations with seventy plus operators. Lenny always seized any opportunity presented, always challenged his company to be bigger and better than it was. His work ethic can be summarized by this: There is no comfort in the growth zone and no growth in the comfort zone.

In *The Bodyguard Blueprint*, Lenny has detailed every step to make an executive protection business successful. I know this because I watched him do it, step by step. He developed a quality product based on exceeding his clients' expectations and through his business acumen and instincts always stayed three steps ahead of the threat and his competition. By setting the standard, Lenny turned International Executive Protection from a company to a brand.

Lenny brings to the table a strong desire to be a master in the world of EP work and to help his students be successful in their individual businesses; a reflection of his role as a Tae Kwon Do master. The instructions he gives in *The Bodyguard Myth* and *The Bodyguard Blueprint* are the exact lessons he has given to hundreds of students from around the world:

"Be a consummate professional, never stop driving forward, believe in yourself, and never quit perfecting your craft." Truly he is the best in the business.

Anthony (Tony) Motley
Chief of Police
Springtown, Texas

Acknowledgments

I would like to thank the people who have stood by me, and have supported my bodyguard classes, and have listened to me. In particularly, I want to thank Adam Montella; Detective Sgt. Tony Motley; Dr. Panagakos; my martial arts instructors; and Master Tommy Carpenter, who has done a phenomenal job teaching tactical gun takeaway and defense.

I would like to thank all my staff and all the people who work with me in IEP. You are outstanding.

I would like to thank three people in particular who have listened to me and followed my blueprint, from three different countries: Aaron French, Deonarine Fluonia, and Brent Eastman.

And I particularly want to thank my parents, who have raised me, always stood beside me, and who have given me a strong moral compass. They are my world.

I would also like to acknowledge my haters who have criticized me, who have put me down, because it only put more fire under my butt to make my company even bigger and better, to outthink them, to outsmart them, to outwork them.

Introduction

Are you ready to put other people to work? With this book, we will address the business end of things to be an executive protection entrepreneur, and the mindset you will need to succeed as a person in business.

In my first book, *The Bodyguard Myth*, we looked at the skill set and mindset you need to be successful as an individual Certified Protection Operator® (CPO). Then we worked on building those skills. In *The Bodyguard Blueprint* we will look at the skill set and mindset of a CEO, the person running a successful executive protection business. We will start by examining the general mindset and then get down to brass tacks. I will introduce some concepts early on, and then expand on them later in more detail.

There's nothing like an active threat to get your attention fully focused in the moment. All the skills you've been honing for years come into play. You're hyper-alert, you're observant, your efforts and movements are synchronized with the rest of the team. And you don't drop your guard even when the emergency has passed.

Most detail work isn't very exciting. We're in the business of avoiding threats, not engaging them. The best detail is the one where "nothing happens." Barely noticed by the client and his companions and not noticed at all by passersby, you observe all comings and goings and constantly plan for all contingencies.

If you can enjoy all aspects of that game, running a business should come naturally. It isn't non-stop excitement. The recognition for a job well done comes mostly from yourself. The rewards are delayed—but they can be great. You'll be assisting the survival of a lot of people: your clients, your team, your family, and their families.

Working for yourself is very different from punching a clock. You'll have slow times and crazy-busy times. The details will be large or small, fun or boring, but never—in my opinion—as dull as being a building security guard. If you've been sitting at a desk on the graveyard shift, the only thing you'll miss when you leave that behind is the steady paycheck.

The question now becomes, what does it take to have a successful CPO business? How do you hire? How do you motivate others to perform at their highest level? How do you keep yourself motivated? How do you market your skills? What are the nuts and bolts of this business? And what sort of characteristics do you need to succeed?

I want the people who become CPOs to now learn to think like CEOs and CFOs (chief financial officers). You have to switch your hat off from bang-bang to writing out a methodical plan, putting a timeline on it, constantly reading it and following through.

"Forever forward" is an important phrase. It means that no matter how small the steps you take, just keep moving forward. Once you stop, or step back, you're losing ground and someone else can come in. You have to keep your motivation and you have to keep your momentum. If you don't, you will fall back or fail.

Business is like a tree. If it's not growing, it's dying. You will need to be very much on top of your business, checking the numbers, making phone calls to people you know, making cold calls, coming up with new ideas. How do we improve the marketing? How do we improve our sales? Where can we save money? Where's the holes in the bucket and how do we fill them to keep the water for us?

How can we better utilize that money that we just saved to grow the business? I'm not talking about investing in a new watch or a new pair of shoes. No. I'm talking about reinvesting it in the company.

If you think "keep it small and take it all," which a lot of people do, you limit yourself. If you "think big," then you will have to think of others. How many families can I feed now? How many more families might I be able to feed in the future? If you think like that, you will have a successful company. When you think of others, you change your responsibility from feeding yourself to feeding your team and their families. The rewards at that level are much greater than just money.

I want you to succeed. My hope is that you'll be able to copy my successful actions—and not my mistakes. This isn't about "being like Lenny." None of it depends on luck or personality. In this book, we're going to talk about actions that are repeatable by anyone with the right mind-set and the right certifications. Let's get started.

1

Why Start an Executive Protection Business?

Before you start a business, you need to know who you are and where you are going. What is your motivation for starting an executive protection business? What are your ultimate goals? Consider your purpose for protecting others. Is it about simply doing something you're good at? Or are you motivated to make a difference in the world?

You will want to decide whether you are doing it to keep it small and take it all, or whether you are thinking beyond yourself, to create something larger that will help more people.

If you have that second idea in mind, how big an effect do you want to create? I firmly believe that with capability comes responsibility. How large a sphere do you want to take responsibility for?

That means, how many people can you employ? Obviously, the higher number of employees means the bigger the company that you have. But with higher numbers comes higher risk and the possibility of higher failure.

How many people can you help on a one-on-one basis? With your business, you should be able to help ten times that many, and for some of you, another ten times. In order to do that, you would have to scale the business upward to be the main provider of executive protection in your area. When people in that area start looking for what you offer, you need to be the one they find.

Why Go into Business for Yourself?

- You want to control your own life, your own thoughts, your own destiny.

- You want the victory of leading a team to a commanding position, and away from danger.
- You can envision a business, staffed by the right people, where you can become prosperous and successful and they provide for their families.
- You are driven to pursue the idea that making money is an art, and keeping money is a science. You must know both.
- You want to take the ceiling off your personal income.
- You want to add a decade or two to your productive life by taking the stress off your body.
- And, of course, you want to have a prosperous retirement by building a retirement fund.

Starting a business sounds like fun, right? And it is. It's fun to land a client, put a detail together, do the detail, work out the kinks, improve on your past successes. But then again, it's not all fun. Waiting for the phone to ring isn't fun. I get it to start ringing any way I can. That gets easier the more postcards you send out, the more hands you shake, and the more people you find who need help.

Pretty soon, through networking and referrals, and a relentless Internet marketing push, a consistent flow will build up and you will be off and running. All these approaches will be discussed in this book.

Success Takes Hard Work

The executive protection industry is not easy, or everybody with some security training would have an agency. Many attempt it and go back to their day jobs, just as a lot of people enroll in college and either drop out or don't use their degree.

It goes back to *intensity of purpose*. Nine people say, "Why try?" and don't think or believe they can accomplish their goals. The tenth person says, "Why not ME?" and starts working on those goals. Day after day he keeps his head down, devouring all the knowledge he can get his hands on, testing and rejecting ideas, keeping what works, and building a lasting business—or empire!

Some, looking from the outside in, only observe the results and call that "exceptional talent." I call it *wanting it bad enough*.

Why not you? If you are reading this book, you are already on your way to transforming your life for the better. The reason I know that is because I did the same thing. I was one of those who asked, "Why not me?" It was really more of a challenge to myself rather than a question. I picked up a book and started reading. Since that first book, I've devoured hundreds of books, audiobooks, seminars, and talks. Hopefully I can help you get there faster by passing on the important lessons I've learned. So please stick with me to the end of this book. I'll make it worth your while.

Successful Traits of an Entrepreneur

Confidence, desire, passion, consistency and work ethic. This is the mindset of a successful entrepreneur. You must be willing to do the backlines work of a business even when you don't feel like it. You elevate your game so that the opposition doesn't stand a chance.

In a fight, you have a known opponent. In business, you have factors that you can control, and factors that are beyond your control. I will briefly mention some things here that you will work on until they are firmly in your control. I will give you an overview here, and get into details later in this book.

Control your own competence. This is a theme I will keep repeating, because it is of key importance. Never stop training. Once you have been my student, you may repeat your classes for free. Stay in practice on the skills you've mastered, and broaden your skill set every chance you get. You can succeed in this business without martial arts training. But the martial arts philosophy has tremendous value to an entrepreneur.

Pay attention to details. Make sure your bids and your agreements are clear and precise. Leaving something open to interpretation could end up in a long, expensive argument between your attorney and the client's attorney.

Run good quality control on your team. This will be fully covered later.

Monitor your alertness. If you have any habits that tend to reduce your alertness, cut them down or cut them out.

Embrace a strong work ethic. I will cover this in much greater detail, summarized by these words:

Whatever can be done today, do it now.

Whatever can be done tomorrow, do it today.

Pay attention to your finances, and reinvest. Actually, someone boiled it down to me one time. They said, *the meaning of* "entrepreneur" is just that *you have enough money to restart if you fail.* And that's the truth. You want to be smart with your money and not lose money, but if the project fails, you must have enough money to keep going forward.

Develop a sound moral compass and operate accordingly. Pay attention whenever your gut is giving you a warning. Compromising in this area is a sure-fire way to take away your drive. I will be talking about this again, particularly how to walk away from sticky situations.

Educate yourself. From a very young age I was always involved in seminars for self-help. I was always involved in learning. I read all kinds of books about business, about entrepreneurship. I would go listen to great speakers, and then challenge myself to be a speaker. Why not me? I wanted to be a part of their circle on the stage, to be like them. So I became a speaker. Doesn't mean I copied what they did. I created my own viewpoint, and then I became that, and then it was just confidence. And I built on that.

My business and professional knowledge came from working around like-minded individuals, who had the same goals I did, or they surpassed my goals and I looked up to them. Because I worked hard and showed promise, they would mentor me. I would look to see what their next move was, and why they thought that way, and then try to utilize that in my business life. I would ask myself, if I did this, how would it turn out?

Then, if it didn't turn out the way I wanted it to, I would ask myself why it didn't turn out the way I had intended.

Never get tripped up by negative emotions. "Know your opponent" is important advice in any business activity. But your opponent may not be just a competitor; it can be the legal red tape that you must be on top of, and the tediousness that goes with mastering that red tape. It could be a distraction in your personal life that gives rise to negative emotions. If you let emotion cloud your vision, or your drive, or your speed, or your belief in yourself, the emotion itself can be considered an opponent.

In a fight, your calculations must be lightning-swift. In a business decision, it may be prudent to let a volatile matter rest until you've sought reliable advice. You can always take a moment to cool down, and act rather than react. Assess these things as objectively as you can and consider before you act.

Success breeds success. Failures should be examined to improve your game plan for next time. Confident people are people who have failed and still know that they are okay. A true entrepreneur is a survivor who can afford to fail and start again. A true entrepreneur isn't someone who waits for opportunity; he goes out and makes opportunities. A true entrepreneur believes in himself.

People want to deal with confident people. As you gain experience, you will build on your successes and learn from your failures; and slowly but surely your confidence will rise.

2

Beginning Your Career

How does an entry-level bodyguard find work or get hired for a job? When I was first starting out, I went to someone and asked, "Can you help me?" And he did. I learned that if people are sincere and altruistic, they will be willing to help. If they say no, be polite, say thank you, and find someone who is willing.

Make yourself noticeable. Make yourself available. Volunteer. Get with someone who already has work and simply ask them to help you. Ask, "Can you help me get a job? Can I be part of your team while I am learning?"

Show interest. Volunteer. Be self-motivated to go to people in the industry and sit down with them and ask, "Is there anything I can do to help you?" It might be something like offering to make sure the vehicle fluids are all topped off for the next detail. It might be checking if there is air in the tires, and if the A/C is running, or starting the vehicle up and see if everything is running well. This is a very basic level of help that you can offer.

Interviewing For Executive Protection Work

Too many resumes come to me that are all about toughness, ability to fight, years in the military. When my office manager presents resumes for my review, those are on the bottom of the pile. Yes, include those things. But your emphasis should be your customer service orientation, your attitude, your versatility in team situations, your willingness to lead.

You have to understand that you are the product that people are going to invest in. *If you don't believe in yourself, then people are not going to believe in you.* How people portray themselves, how they look, how they talk, gives signals in every aspect of their life. So you have to make sure that you are leading the life of a professional, not just a tough guy. You must present yourself as a professional, and operate as a professional.

This will come into play while you're protecting the client. It's equally important to protect your image and your company's image. Negative reviews spread ten times farther and faster than glowing reviews. So the image you present will be a key factor.

My First Experiences as an EP Agent

The first thing I learned was that everything changes in the industry. It is always moving. The threats change. People get sick. People leave the team. New people come on the team. More threats come, more threats go. So part of the skill set is to develop an awareness of and ability to adapt to change.

The second thing I learned was to watch for red flags. Listen to how a potential client is wording how they want security. When people say they want a bodyguard, that is a red flag, because not many people ask for a bodyguard unless they are under direct, immediate threat. People will ask for an escort, security, something in a less intense way than, "I need a bodyguard. "They will say, "I need professional assistance.""I need somebody who can watch my daughter or my children.""I am having a problem and I am in fear of this happening. Is there anybody who can watch my home while this is happening?" Things like that.

If they ask if I have bullet-proof vests, and can I look more militant and tacked out, that is a red flag. Yeah, we can do that. But ask why? If the answer is that there are gang members shooting, then I don't want the job, because now they are trying to make me a bigger bully than the assholes who are out there. That would be unprofessional of me.

If they said, "This is what I need because this is what I'm up against," then I would come up with a way of protecting them without going force-to-force with other people who don't care who they hurt or when they hurt them. That would be very foolish, and I wouldn't do that. I learned that very quickly.

Conceiving a Purpose

You have to have a purpose that drives you. Purpose is what powers your engine. Otherwise, you go nowhere.

As a young man, I worked as a lifeguard for some years at the Long Center in Clearwater, Florida. As well as being a premier public athletic center, it also houses UPARC (Upper Pinellas Association for Retarded Citizens). Next to the Olympic-size pool was a rehab center for special-needs children. Many were in wheelchairs or walkers, unable to jump or run—and delighted just to be outside. And there I was at the peak of athleticism, taking my gifts for granted.

I asked myself this: *Why me?* God had blessed me, but I had reached a low point and wasn't using my talent to the fullest. After watching these children with extreme challenges year in and year out, I conceived a purpose that became a motivating force: let *me* fight for those kids, be their champion. I could see I was not living to my full potential, that I was squandering this blessing. So I decided to take all of my positive energy, and the blessings from God, and put them to work in the right direction. This became my burning desire, which turned my passion into a driving force.

I found a way to lead myself out of my own doldrums by working for a higher purpose, and leadership skills followed. I worked on developing a sincere, altruistic state of mind: wanting to win for the kids who could not walk, talk, or jump, or play. It became a part of me to always be willing to give back in various ways, to find meaning and motivation in helping the people who cannot help themselves, in helping the weak and picking them up.

I decided to win the World Games for them. I turned the question "Why me?" around to "Why not me?" Each time I saw those kids, I tried to step up my Taekwondo game a little further. I felt I was fighting for the kids, competing for them.

If you can find a purpose like that, turn it into an advantage as I did. Having a purpose is a source of energy.

I discovered, as well, that I had another driving purpose, which was to help those around me to succeed.

After winning the World Games, I took that second purpose and worked with students for 20 years with my own martial arts school. Over those years, I became good friends with many professionals in the military and law enforcement. I taught seminars in Hapkido, Jiu Jndividuals inn martial arts andmyself in my TaekwonddoJJjjjjitsu, women's self-defense, and taught Kid Safe seminars.

I also created the magazine *MMA Authority* and ran it profitably for years. As publisher, I often found it necessary to arrange security for photoshoots and other events involving MMA fighters and models. Given my martial arts background, it was only natural that I took on the security role myself.

I got used to dealing with SWAT and other trained people. Using my martial arts training and philosophy, I found that I was able to guide and improve the mental game plan of those professionals, to share ideas, and to improve my own approach to security in the process. Since that time, I have trained SWAT teams nationally and internationally, as well as other defense forces. I have never stopped the learning process.

In 2009, I founded International Executive Protection LLC (IEP), to work with those who are serious about a career in executive protection or serious about increasing their skills. We offer to our students a world-class, hands-on, comprehensive training and certification program for executive protection, special operations and bodyguard training. My classes evolve continuously. They have grown from local to national to global—to the Caribbean Islands, and now I am lucky to teach in Europe.

I've always loved teaching self-defense, close-quarter combat, hand-to-hand, martial arts. As security equipment and practices have evolved, it has become interesting to teach the same art to people who are leading teams with riot gear, weapons, guns, OC (pepper) sprays, and other equipment.

I have trained with many instructors who were phenomenally talented and skilled. Among those were a few who either didn't know how to communicate their talent or were not yet team players. That taught me yet another lesson—that when I teach, my motivation comes from that same burning desire to make my students great.

This constantly demands that I give my best. Whether I do that directly affects my students. It is true for me that if a leader, team lead, or other person only gives 80% of their energy, the class, students, and team will give around 60% and no higher than 75%. To truly be a leader, this is what is required—a 100% effort.

So this is how I started. I developed my purpose. I got to know myself and found what drove me, what moved me forward, and I built my life around that. I constantly worked on competence, and I was ready when opportunity presented itself. As my training and experience kept growing and growing, the learning process kept going and going as well. It became easier and easier to envision the steps to take to accomplish these goals.

Find your purpose and keep it in sight. Keep growing your competence. Keep the learning process going. The steps to accomplish your goals will become evident.

Sacrifice Has Its Limits

How much will you sacrifice to attain your business goals?

You may have to sacrifice the unrealistic expectations of your family and friends. If they're used to a predictable routine, that may be one of the first things to go. You're going to be working a job *and* a business for a while—possibly a year or two. Get your friends and family members to buy into this new operating basis.

Here is the typical sequence to transition from working for others to operating successfully on your own. It is not an overnight process:

1) A job.
2) A job and a side business.
3) A business and a side job.
4) A business.
5) A career.

That's what works and wins, unless you also have an inheritance or a rich uncle who wants to invest. Either way, it is a lot of work. It is a lot of sacrifice of time and energy.

While success does take commitment and sacrifice, it is important to take a breather from taking things seriously. Give yourself some time off every week. Work hard, but also play hard. Enjoy outings with family and friends; kill time doing nothing.

Even during the most grueling stages of the transition, leave something stable and predictable in your schedule for the people who like to hang out with you. Pizza night with the family might be Tuesday instead of Saturday, but give them something they can count on.

This gets trickier if you're sharing kids with an ex-spouse, but you have to do it.

It may appear lopsided, like 90% work and 10% fun. Work on the *quality* of your time together and it will show and be appreciated.

Admittedly, I struggle with this all the time. I am constantly in work mode. It is very hard for me to stop thinking of the next goal, the next project, the next detail, because I absolutely love what I do. I am always happy to meet new people, make new friends, and secure people's lives, family, property, and belongings. If you don't love what you do, you will never be able to enjoy the fruits of your labor.

Excellence Is a Habit

As Will Durant wrote in a discussion of the great Greek philosopher Aristotle: "…we are what we repeatedly do. Excellence, then, is not an act but a habit."

So let me give you your first goal: to create a habit. Finish this book! As you read, I suggest that you bookmark the pages containing instructions you'll want to refer to later.

Good Customer Service

What will set you apart from the competition? For me, it is customer service, second to none, end of story. It is a key differentiator.

Customer service in the executive protection field means how well and how quickly you respond. I will show you how I operate.

First, a live person picks up the phone.

Second, I have a network of contacts that is amazing and always expanding, so I can quickly field the best team available. I can staff a detail with female bodyguards, inconspicuous bodyguards, guards who wear a suit naturally and don't draw attention to their awesomeness.

Third, I will be getting done all the advance work needed for a successful deployment.

I'm always looking to deploy a team rather than *be* the team. As much as I love detail work, I'm going to stay in the office generating more business if at all possible.

I call it "working *on* my business rather than *in* my business."

With all the competitors out there, how do you differentiate yourself? What makes you stand out? Everyone is going to say the same stuff: "I can protect you, we have this, we have that, we have one thing or another." What's the difference with me? Customer service. It is my approach, my follow up, my follow through, my sense of urgency.

What makes you different?

Manage Your Wealth

How you manage your money will make or break you, so this is something you need to plan from the earliest stages of your business. *The Richest Man in Babylon* by George Samuel Clason has been one of the most influential books in my life, and I recommend reading this book. Here are some important lessons I learned from him. These lessons should be learned early on and incorporated from the beginning of your career to the end:

- Have a reliable income stream.
- Crush the spirit of procrastination within you.
- Don't confuse desires with actual needs. Your"necessary expenses" will grow to match your income unless you resist that urge.
- Pay yourself first by saving at least 10 percent of everything you earn.
- Clason says, "Then learn to make your treasure work for you. Make it your slave. Make its children and its children's children work for you." I did this by buying small houses.
- Own your home.
- Avoid investments that sound too good to be true.

If you spend more than you make, you'll bottom out. If you are in debt, live on 70% of what you make. Save 10% for yourself. Use the remaining 20% to repay your debts.

I took these lessons to heart. In the beginning, I worked very hard to make money, but I saved every dollar. I lived in the same house for 23 years, in a very small house. But I ended up with 23 investment properties. When the housing bubble burst years ago, my real estate investments were all paid for.

I bought a home; I paid it off as fast as I could. I bought a second home. I took the money from the first home and put it into the second home. I took the money from the first two and bought a third, and kept repeating this process. I have other investments as well.

I always have asked myself, "What's my end goal?" and then have taken the steps to accomplish that end goal. Because of that, I'm in a good situation financially, and this is what I recommend to you.

3

Three Branches of
Executive Protection

Executive production has three distinct branches, and each offers opportunities. To get more work, it helps to be skilled and licensed in these three disciplines:

- executive protection
- private investigation
- security (such as building security and event security).

I have discussed the nuts and bolts of these disciplines in *The Bodyguard Myth.*

Others' perception of your business is governed by how you position your business. If you position yourself as an EP specialist, EP clients will seek you out in preference to a "security" company. On other communication channels, yes, you are a security company, and you have references to prove it.

At the beginning, any detail that utilizes your bodyguard skills or your team management skills is a prize to be pursued and won.

In executive protection work, you're protecting individual lives. You're giving celebrities that rarest commodity: *an uneventful day.*

As with security work, you're securing a perimeter—but not a fixed perimeter such as an event venue.

In executive protection, the perimeter is like a moving box around the client. Smooth movement is accomplished by every team member guarding his section of the perimeter while taking responsibility for the overall success of the mission.

Lenny Bogdanos

We offer private investigation (PI) for people who say, "I think my wife or husband is cheating on me" and ask us to go do an investigation. We'll do it and have the PI licenses to do it. But that's not what we primarily focus on. If they said, "I have a client coming to town; he's a very wealthy person who holds information about the next life-saving drug, and people want to take his patent or intellectual information," then I'll have a PI understand everything about him and the threat. I will monitor where he's staying, so I can see when people go in and out.

We learn to think like the threat in order to contain the threat. For example, if I wanted to breach a compound, I would watch it. I would know when the guards change, when the gates open, when other guards come and go. I would watch to see when the workers come in, when maintenance comes in, pool companies come in, the cooks come in, church groups come in. And then I would understand, "OK, on Wednesday there's church from 6:00-7:00 p.m. in this compound, or this secured facility. Every morning they open the gate at 5:00 a.m. for the cook. At 6:00 a.m. they open the gate for this person. At 7:30 a.m. they open up the main gate because they want to get the newspaper to bring to the client." I start profiling that threat and taking notes, because here's the big thing: when the gate opens, the threat can piggyback in, and then they are inside.

We do this internally, and we call it "doing an advance." To have a PI who does it and can methodically write it out and understand it always helps. They may call it something else, but in the bodyguard industry, we call it "an advance."

Is private investigation a minor part of the business? For me it is. However, to be able to do private investigation is crucial to profiling the client and profiling the threat. You have to investigate what the threat is: is it high-threat, low-threat, high-risk, low-risk?

But also it's very important that you profile your client. Are they lying? *When people lie, people die.* If I'm talking to a client and they lie to me, not only are they putting their own lives in jeopardy, they're putting my life and my team's life on the line. If I'm working a detail and my partner, or buddy, doesn't give me the proper information, or if he didn't gather it properly and he lies to me, someone can get hurt.

Underestimating the threat, minimizing the threat level, not doing a thorough investigation, can have a very bad outcome. Private investigators, if they don't do a thorough check and just say that they did, can have a bad outcome.

Case in point: A client is an abused woman. I ask, "The person who beat you (her husband), does he have any weapons?""Yeah, he's got a couple weapons.""Okay, does he have a hot head?""Yes, he's got a very bad temper." Now you want to investigate who he is, profile him. So if she says that he only has a couple of guns and then I find out that, no, he has a whole cache of guns—ARs, AKs, sawed-off shotguns, etc.—I have averted a potentially lethal situation. I need to know the facts. So if she minimizes it because she says that those are *her* guns, I have to read between the lines.

Case in point: The advance team reports back to me what they claim to be the whole scene, including the choke points and where the safe room is and that it is secured for the client. I take somebody in an emergency situation to the safe room, but find out that I need management to unlock that door. That safe room was not, in fact, secured. Either the advance wasn't thorough enough, or they lied to me.

Private investigation details can lead to protection details, and vice versa. So it makes good marketing sense to be able to promote this capability.

4

Think Like a CEO

When you decide to create your own business, you are automatically promoting yourself to the position of chief executive officer—the CEO. You are at the top of your organizational chart. You are the number one person in your business (chief). You are the one creating and executing plans and orders (executive), and you are the one in command (officer).

A CEO is in it for the long haul. Unlike a Certified Protection Operator (CPO), the CEO is never off duty. His free time is spent building a future for the team members and the organization. A CPO is only a CPO when carrying out a detail. The CPO gets the assignment, the briefing, hits the switch and *bam!* Fully engaged. When it's over, he hits the switch again and it's over.

But when you've got your own agency or are an International Executive Protection (IEP) affiliate, when the detail is over, you put on your CEO hat and get on with building your business.

If you are affiliated with IEP, then you have the advantage. The IEP system works around the world—what I teach, how I teach it, what I say, how I say it. These are all part of a system that works: our level of training as a CPO and CEO, how to brand yourself, how to market yourself, how to conduct yourself.

Components of Success

Success as a CPO requires all these components:

- stamina
- persistence
- patience
- tolerance of inaction as well as action.

As a CEO, you'll need the first three qualities, plus these:

- people skills
- ability to switch hats rapidly
- ability to see things from the other person's viewpoint
- dedication to the success of your whole company and team.

As a CEO, you won't see much inaction, because you'll jump on marketing whenever things aren't moving. Whenever you get a breather, you'll go into planning mode, review your written goals and add to them.

To succeed as a CEO, you'll need persistence and patience a hundred times over. You also have to be driven. And when you're driven, you'll sometimes get frustrated with paperwork, red tape—anything that slows you down.

If you are smart, you are going to be measuring your production by the numbers (see the list of things to measure later in this chapter in the section, "Statistics"). This is covered in *The Bodyguard Myth* as well. If the numbers are not moving in the right direction, you're going to do something about it. Don't be too hard on yourself in the process. Breathe.

The CEO Mindset

Many people get stuck in repeating the things that have worked for them in the past: "I am a bodyguard," "I am a trained machine." Great, you know that, but that's not how you present yourself to prospective clients. They want to meet the boss—a confident businessman who can field a great team on a moment's notice.

Even if it's a one-person detail, bring your CEO mindset to the table. You're going to field a great team, even if it's a team of one. Clients need certainty that you have resources to expand the team without missing a beat, that you have others who can be trusted with the command in case of emergency.

You're selling peace of mind. You're selling a trouble-free day or week, a distraction-free event or appearance, an unobtrusive security presence (soft target) or a presence the bad guys don't want to mess with (hard target). What you are selling adds up to the best experience possible, backed by the best team possible.

At the start of your executive protection business, you don't have a marketing department or a board of directors. *You* are every department head, as well as the boss they answer to. Ask yourself:

- Am I writing down my 3-month and 6-month goals?
- Am I setting a timeline to achieve my goals?
- Am I taking charge and making the big decisions?
- Am I taking advantage of opportunities that come up?
- Am I enjoying hard work and effort for its own sake, even at the expense of comfort and convenience?

The point of this exercise is to start thinking like a CEO. You MUST be willing to diligently pursue each of these points. Focus your mind and energy on building your company to gain financial independence. Be prepared to beat your competition to the deal on a Sunday afternoon. Make decisions that make sense for the long term, whatever the inconvenience in the short term.

CEOs plan ahead. Where will your company be in five years? Get that vision as clearly as you can and name the broad, general steps it will take to get there. Obviously, you can't predict in detail what the world will throw in your path, but if you are powering forward toward a known goal, the world will have a tendency to step out of your way.

Your Daily Routine

Establish a consistent daily routine that is healthy for mind and body, and stick to it.

What time does your workday start? Start it at the same time every day, and once it starts, handle only business. Get your personal calls and emails out of the way either before your workday starts or after it ends. Compartment the workday. You might have a period for answering emails, followed by a period for outbound calls and outbound emails and a period for other marketing activities. Once your business day has started, don't answer texts or emails of a non-urgent nature. If you set aside an hour for outbound calls, do outbound calls. Talk to prospects or clients if they call, but no one else.

ake phin things. I wouldn' don'really only do indicators. But when'fore it reaches You can be most efficient by setting up a routine so you handle a certain kind of traffic at the same time every day. Then you can handle a lot of that one thing. The worst approach is what I call the "reactive" approach, meaning that you wait for the environment to tell you what to do next. If nobody is demanding something, you just sit there stupefied. Your sales will never get off the ground if you take the reactive approach. Be proactive!

When you're scheduling sales interviews, consider the customer's convenience first and foremost, but disrupt your own routine as little as possible. And when you do set appointments, send a calendar invite. You can use the Google Calendar app on both your phone and computer, and it will automatically synchronize. You don't need a Gmail account to use Google Calendar, but a Gmail account is great if you want free email, word processing and spreadsheets. If you want to understand better how Gmail Apps work, some public libraries offer a course in that. Google also has a G Suite Learning Center at gsuite.google.com where you can take a number of tutorials.

Reporting Is Key

Reporting is key. We always should *inspect what we expect.*

No matter how good somebody is at a task I've delegated, I need accurate reports from the field. No news is definitely bad news when an update is due. Boots on the ground are nothing without eyes 360 degrees.

If you're not sure what to believe, inspect the scene personally.

I can't do my job without good intel coming in at all times from all sources. That includes making time to check my news feeds about threat intelligence in the sectors I'm helping to protect.

Again, the job of a CEO is not to do the work himself (unless it's unavoidable). It's mainly to coordinate the work of others, to monitor indicators (those signs that show—or indicate—how things are going) and step in when needed. The key indicators for an executive to watch are his organization's production statistics.

Statistics

When I first start working with people, I often ask them about their goals. Many people in this business live week to week, paycheck to paycheck. They think about tomorrow, maybe next week. If they set goals, these are often small, because they aren't used to aiming higher, and haven't adjusted their expectations accordingly.

Think BIG! You can't achieve big results if you don't believe in big results. You have to aim high to reach a high level of performance. If you aim for the bronze, you likely won't make it, so aim for the gold every time. To achieve BIG, you have to think even BIGGER.

Visualize your goal. A ship without a rudder has no direction. You are the rudder. You are the steering mechanism in the ship that is your life. Steer yourself in a specific direction. Be as definite as possible about what you are trying to achieve.

Develop statistical measures you can use to monitor your weekly or monthly progress toward the goal. Is your income going up or down? Are you receiving more calls or fewer than last week or the week before? How many business cards did you hand out this week? Keeping these numbers will tell you what is working, and where you need more effort.

Record these things, tally them up. Graph the more important ones. It all has to be measurable. If you want to make your money back, keep track of the numbers and act accordingly.

Here are some meaningful statistics that aren't difficult to calculate and keep track of:

- dollar value of deals closed
- sales phone calls made
- sales phone calls received
- sales phone calls converted to appointments
- business cards handed out
- letters and postcards mailed out systematically.

Also, you must count the responses from letters and postcards that are mailed out to see how effectively you are marketing. If you're marketing at a high level, you're going to get about a 1% to 3% return on every 100 or 1000 postcards that you put out. This means your message has to be clear and well thought out when you do direct mail marketing, laying out exactly what you do, so that people feel comfortable with your services.

You don't need more than a few key statistics. Keep track. Add them up for the week or month and graph them. Post the graphs near your desk and always work at pushing those statistics up. You will know from your statistics if you need to change something or if what you are doing is succeeding.

Tackle It Now

There is no better time than now to make things happen. So many times, people put things off because they think they can start tomorrow.

Start today. Start right now. Start by writing down a goal. Start by writing down a deadline.

Are there some parts of the job you avoid because they're too tedious— not fun—and yet they're necessary? Tackle them first. There's a small victory just in overcoming your own resistance and getting that task started. There's a payoff when you get it done, because then you can move on to the next thing, which is a bit more fun.

Here are some reasons you might not like to do a particular task:

1) You're not good at it.
2) You don't really understand it.

Let's face it, #2 is usually the reason for #1. All the more reason to tackle it now. Google what you don't understand, get it clarified. If it is a complex task, take a class that covers it. Find a tutorial online. And once you understand it, pat yourself on the back for a job well done.

Make Those Outbound Calls

Do not procrastinate. If you do, you are simply putting off your own success. If something looks hard to do, do something harder. If you're not feeling the urgency, invent some.

Don't stare at the phone inventing reasons why it's not the best time to call. Pick up the phone and dial. Know what you're going to say when they pick up. Know what the next step is toward a deal and move it along every time. If an obstacle comes up, find out what can be done to move that obstacle out of the way, and ask for the business.

You will very often have your call be routed to voicemail. When that happens, leave short voicemails that ask a question. Pay attention and always leave your contact information.

Stay hungry. Be hungry now and stay hungry ten years from now. Keep that drive and motivation by never being fully satisfied and remaining humble.

The Skill of Multitasking

When I hear someone say, "I'm not good at multitasking," I know they don't understand what the word means. Multitasking is a mental skill.

We only have two hands and two feet; we can only do so much with our physical bodies. But with our minds, we should be able to think outside the box, delegate, and think of multiple things to get the job done.

When you multitask, you have to use your mind in many different directions:

- understand your team
- talk to your team
- understand your client
- listen to your client
- think ahead three or four steps.

That is a person who can multitask: he can separate his attention into multiple areas and get the job done without losing sight or focus of the principal/client, the health of the team, and the final destination.

Being a multitasker also means that you're able to work remote locations and ensure that people in any part of the world are working in sync with what you want them to do.

Having said all this, there is a key principle that must be understood for successful multitasking: You only have attention for one thing at a time. That may sound like a contradiction, but it isn't. If you want to get nothing done at all, try doing two or three things at the exact same moment. If you want to lose business, answer phone calls and texts while you're talking to a prospective client. Give each task your full attention as you are doing it.

I don't like distractions. I give my undivided attention to one thing at a time. However, by making decisions quickly and delegating effectively, I can be managing a long list of people and activities at any given time. Learn to make correct decisions fast and it will become obvious to others that you're a "good multitasker."

Delegate

Most people who appear to multitask effectively are good at delegating and scheduling. If you have ten people working on individual tasks that add up to an overall target, there's your multitasking. That's you keeping your eye on the ball and making sure your plan unfolds on schedule.

When people are ready for responsibility, delegate some. That frees up your attention to work toward long-range accomplishments. Let the rising stars on your team make a name for themselves too. If they end up surpassing your accomplishments, that's all to your credit. "Your success is my success" is a viewpoint that works. Encourage them to set up their own business, but discourage them from setting it up in your backyard.

When I delegate, I have to make sure I'm delegating to the right person for the right job. It's the same thing that I teach in class. I talk about how the situation is going to determine the tactics.

In addition to finding the right person for a job and letting them get on with it, you can also "delegate" tasks to computers. Only with the Internet can you create a marketing machine that generates qualified leads while you sleep.

Be an Inspiration

This is something I try to do. Being an inspiration truly means motivating people. That's it. If I can motivate somebody to get off their butt and take my class, and they listen to me, and they're not lazy when I'm not in front of them, they will become successful. They have to be motivated. I love to motivate people. When people take my classes, whether it's Level 1 or Level 2—Beginner or Advanced—I always motivate each and every student, individually and collectively. I have done this for years: motivated people to compete and win. I motivate people to start businesses and companies. I motivate people around the world to think big and have broad ideas with broad shoulders. This is how you stay on the top.

In order to motivate others, you need to stay motivated yourself. You don't let people bring you down or threaten you or try to strip you of your dreams. You have to stay strong. Stay alert. Stay on point. Once you lose motivation, get out of the game. It's over. If you always have a burning desire inside of you, you will become successful.

Choose confidence over cockiness. Instead of being cocky and looking down on others, be humble and people will look up to you and respect you. In my experience, arrogant people are out of touch with reality. They are all talk and no substance. You don't need to lower yourself to their level, but sometimes—just by being real and setting a good example—you can inspire them to be better.

In all of my classes, I pre-frame the students—give them a set of guidelines and expectations about attitude—and motivate them as much as possible. I teach them at the highest level possible, at their saturation rate, the amount they can retain, before I move on. That is one thing as an instructor that I have learned over years of training people. I have trained people at the highest levels, whether it has been martial arts, self-defense, women's self-defense, tactical shooting, formations, executive protection. But I don't move on until I see that it has all soaked in. I teach it, we go over it, then we go to something different, then we come back.

What I don't want is for a student to get stuck in a bad habit. It is like a kid learning to ride a bike. If he keeps falling down—seven, eight, nine times—let's stop for a minute. Let's go get some Kool-Aid. And let's get back on it. Break that bad cycle. Because once they get stuck in that bad cycle, it's not good. So we just keep moving forward, and changing it, and then going back to it and reinforcing what we did.

If someone is lacking in confidence, I try to build them up. I use the formula called PCP—praise, correct, praise—which I will discuss later. I try to never demean people or put them down. I always try to lift them up. Being an inspiration is very important to me, and I take it very seriously.

From the ground up, I want to build people to be strong. Stripping them of their self-esteem and pride is not the right way to do it. By guiding them and helping them, and making them feel comfortable, you will have a much better student, team member, or worker.

A true leader inspires people to be greater than they are. He sets a good example and shares the wisdom gained by the experience of aggressively pursuing goals and learning from and actually becoming better with every setback.

A good team player makes teammates better. A good coach is willing for players to attain their greatness and become leaders in their own right.

Learn by Teaching

I found a passion in teaching, training, speaking and making people believe in themselves. I found this passion after pursuing my Olympic dreams. On that journey, I learned countless lessons on life, discipline, and work ethic.

This won't work for everyone, but I do encourage everyone to try it: explaining how to do something is a great way to put your thoughts in order. It also brings your uncertainties into view and makes you do something about them. It is one of the best ways to increase your own competence and certainty.

Mastering the Opposition

In every detail there is a known or theoretical opponent. However, as I told you in *The Bodyguard Myth*, our strategy is to avoid engagement by outsmarting the opponent. This is unlike military or law enforcement, where the strategy is to seek out and neutralize the opponent.

Be greater than your competitors. Be a class act. Don't run down the competition in a sales interview; more often than not, it backfires.

On a detail, our job is to maintain an orderly perimeter that threats can't penetrate. The potential opponent is not just an aggressor, but could be a photographer, an overeager fan, or a publicity seeker. If they're not someone the client wants to deal with, they're somebody we want to keep at a safe distance.

In business, we also have a perimeter to maintain. You've conquered a certain amount of territory, you've established a position in the pecking order. Put up a map and mark the outer reaches of your potential territory with gold map tacks. Use your imagination. This could be anywhere that you know at least one CPO who could take on a detail, or one referral source who can generate business for you there.

There are several ways to expand your territory. Defending your perimeter would mean getting all the repeat business you can, doing a great job for every client you get, stabilizing your work force by making them feel appreciated and bringing out their best in the way you assign specialties and in the way you train a team and communicate with them.

When you meet another EP professional in your territory, assume first that the person is a potential ally. Add them to your network. When work becomes available, somebody else may find out about it first; make sure they think of you if they need additional staffing.

In business, beware of the real opposition: it is what you have a responsibility to do, but aren't doing. This may be your lack of a plan or a predictable, comprehensive schedule. It may be a lack of some knowledge or a limitation of your own capabilities—or it may be just you running yourself down.

My rule about that last is: don't do it. If you find yourself being negative about your abilities or potential, find something positive to focus on. Later in this book, I will cover the subject of affirmations, which has been a key factor for my success. I can't overstate the importance of keeping your goals and affirmations fresh in your mind.

It is your personal responsibility to keep a positive self-image.

Of course, you're constantly overcoming the "opposition" of time and money limitations, the limitations of your own endurance, people who try your patience, government red tape and other business and financial obstacles.

Let's talk about an opponent that comes from within your organization, and what to do about it. This opponent is the unwilling subordinate who always knows best. What I need is simple and easy: do what I ask, listen to what I say, follow instructions, don't leave your post, and stay on the detail.

But there will be some who don't want to listen. They will try to outthink me; they will try to think bigger and better. These are the people who will try to dismantle the people around them: they will be mean to them, belittle them, and hurt them in some way, shape or form. These are the people who bring you down, who are obstructionists, who usually consider themselves victims. But they are only victims in their own mind. And they try to make their victim status so known that everybody has to talk about it.

There's no place for this in my company or on my team. I don't need people around me who are self-caused victims. Too many people are victims. They whine about this, they don't have that, they don't have a daddy. So many reasons why people are victims, but let's just grow up, get over it, and move on.

In understanding your opponents, the wisdom of Sun-Tzu, who wrote the book *The Art of War* 2500 years ago, can truly elevate your thinking about how to overcome obstacles. Apply this to the list of opponents I just mentioned:

- *"Hence to fight and conquer in all your battles is not supreme excellence; supreme excellence consists in breaking the enemy's resistance without fighting."* Be so well prepared that the threat will see a hard target even if not dressed that way. Break down their plans, impede their progress to defeat us.
- *"Therefore the skillful leader subdues the enemy's troops without any fighting; he captures their cities without laying siege to them; he overthrows their kingdom without lengthy operations in the field."* Win deals by having the best reputation. Don't run the competition down.
- *"Thus the highest form of generalship is to balk the enemy's plans."*
- *"If you know the enemy and know yourself, you need not fear the result of a hundred battles."* This is an exercise in visualization. Can you think like someone who is plotting to embarrass your client, disrupt his presentation, attack him from behind on the stage? When I was competing athletically, I would study my opponents. By seeing them, studying their moves, learning their strengths and weaknesses, I could understand them better and anticipate their moves. I also study my competition, including their

marketing materials, and I also study the threats. I understand and anticipate their moves and actions.

- *"In all fighting, the direct method may be used for joining battle, but indirect methods will be needed in order to secure victory."* For the John Andrew Welden detail, which I covered in *The Bodyguard Myth*, I used a decoy vehicle to attract the media and protestors while we took Andrew around the back in a second vehicle.
- *"To secure ourselves against defeat lies in our own hands, but the opportunity of defeating the enemy is provided by the enemy himself."* If a competitor waits a day or two to respond to a time-sensitive lead, I'm already there running the detail.

You have to understand your opponents—all of them. When it comes to the threats to your clients, you profile them. This is not racial profiling. You profile their characteristics, their movements, their daily activities, their social media behavior. That allows you to make a better threat assessment, and then you can make better decisions to improve your company. Don't forget to also deal with the internal threats, whether it is an employee with a counter-productive attitude, or you allowing a bad self-image to sneak through the gates.

Competition

We'll come back to this again and again. Who is bidding for the same work in your geographic area? Consider them part of your network and get to know them. Any "competitor" is a potential resource. They might hire you in the future, or you might hire them.

There are some you'll learn to steer clear of. There are some who may run you down in an effort to get the business. Get to know them and defeat their negative actions strategically, not head to head. Be better than they are and prove it through your actions. Lead by example.

There's an old rule in sales: *don't knock the competition.* It reflects badly on the critic—usually worse than on the one being criticized. You're bigger than that.

Correct approach: "I lead the industry in _____ " (if you are). "Just ask_____."

Your competition will mainly come from the lowest bidder. Be willing to lose that bid if the deal wouldn't be profitable. I provide the highest level of service at an affordable price. Not everyone can afford me.

How will I price my product compared to my competition? Don't decrease prices, increase value. Be sure you start out with a proper meeting and express your value. Use stories and testimonials to illustrate your skills and customer service. Demonstrate your superior knowledge and genuine desire to help that individual.

What Not to Do

Here's a bad way to start, and it happens in every one-on-one service industry. It's called, "Let's cut out the middleman."

I have friends who are happy to work under me on a detail, if I have won the business. And if they win some business, they can include me in the detail or subcontract the whole detail to me. That's a friendly arrangement: we're all out there hustling, and we have our own networks, our own referral sources, and we all make sure the work gets done and the client is happy.

If you're the middleman—the person who is putting the team together—you stay in business by adding value, by being able to field the best team the fastest. Subcontractors who would cut you out are not really your friends anyway, so don't put them in a position where they would be tempted. Make your agreements very explicit.

Tell your subs that if a client approaches them to cut out the middleman, they must report it to you. Why? While they're on the detail, you're doing the marketing, the networking and the calls to generate more business. This is to everyone's benefit. Executive protection is a relatively small industry, and word gets around. If a subcontractor cuts you out, you'll cut them off, and the rest of your network will hear about it.

There's a saying, "Give a man a fish, feed him for a day; teach a man to fish, feed him for a lifetime." I'd like to expand on that: I will give you a fish, and then I'll show you how to fish, but don't take my fishing pole. It's very important, because there has been the occasional person who has tried to do that to me. I taught them, I gave them an opportunity, and they went right behind my back to try to take my clients. Don't touch my pole.

Keep Your Work Life Enjoyable

If the work isn't fun, a motivation to make money alone will not be enough to make you stay with it. The first few setbacks will push you toward something that is easier, something you're already used to doing. And what good is that? Drawing a predictable paycheck that evaporates before it reaches your bank account?

Be focused without getting too serious, too solid. You want your attention to be focused, not fixated. An opportunity could be sitting right in front of you. You won't miss it if you're focused.

You can get too fixated on a problem and be unable to solve it. If you can keep a light-hearted approach to something, solutions appear.

Executive protection is hard work, but it's also fun when you have a good team that works together well. If you hire a superstar who isn't a team player, who wants to impress others with their toughness, look out. You probably won't do it a second time.

As you get to know your teams, you'll begin to gravitate to the same names over and over again. You'll become more and more relaxed with that core group and to have fun with them, while keeping enough professional distance to keep their respect.

Cultivate a Winning Spirit

The biggest reason for my success is that I was never afraid to fail. *The only real failure is giving up.* With that being said, I love to win. That is my spirit: winning. The number one thing that I absolutely hate is to lose. I am a winner by nature, and a champion at heart. It is this combination that has brought me to the pinnacle of the EP industry. With my marketing and my relentless pursuit of goals—while thinking outside the box—I have grown in multiple countries and surpassed multiple companies.

I embraced each setback as a lesson on the road to success. This is what made me a world champion and a business success. I also believed in never letting people down. This is especially true in business, where other people's welfare is always involved.

I have worked very hard, put others before myself, and been willing to sacrifice in many ways so that I could achieve my goals. I don't just have personal goals; I have goals for the groups I belong to, whose success—or even survival—depends on what I do.

5

Coaching Yourself Forward

I want to expose you to certain positive habits that have been backbones to my success.

Belief is a habit. If you tell yourself something often enough, it becomes reality. That's certainly true of any negative thing you think about yourself. I'm not saying, "Stop doing that." I know you would if it were that simple. No, my advice is to take over the mindspace that is occupied with repetitions of the negative, and fill that space with positive affirmations, visualizations and goal setting.

We will be looking in depth at all three, and they will become your three main tools to keep the fuel in the tank and your foot on the gas pedal instead of the brakes.

The Power of Visualization

If you do what you have always done, you will get what you have always gotten.

The number one reason people fail or never succeed at a high level is because they think small, and believe success is impossible. They may become a jack-of-all-trades and never master one thing.

I am going to challenge you to take over something that you do all the time automatically, and that is your power of visualization. Your will and your imagination are tools with which you make your destiny.

There's one thing anyone can do, but hardly anybody does: *write down your goals, including when you want them accomplished*. Then visualize them done.

Keep them handy. You can use a pocket-sized notebook or an app on your phone. Post it on the fridge, mirror, iPad, etc.

It's not complicated. Make a list; grow and refine it over time. Think of the list as a living and breathing document. Read the goals aloud once a day. Look at them anytime you need a "reset," like taking out a compass and finding north again.

Have a date in mind for a milestone you want to attain. Visualize that date and visualize yourself already in possession of what it is you want.

I cannot overstate the importance of grooving in this habit and not losing it.

Visualize yourself closing the deal, buying a home or another investment property. Visualize yourself in the mental state you want to be in. That's a trick, because you have to step outside the mental state you are in now. Do this at a quiet time when there are no outside demands on your attention.

Success starts in your mind. It starts with visualization. We all have to start from somewhere and improve on that condition. To paraphrase Napoleon Hill, if you can believe it and conceive it, you can achieve it. *Visualize your hard work paying off.*

Here is a quick question that I will expand upon in a later chapter. If you can make $15K a year, $30K a year, $60K a year, why can't you double it? You can't just lie on the sofa and visualize yourself in a mansion with a Lamborghini in the driveway unless you have a methodical outlook with a realistic goal and visualize it step by step.

During the day, there's a lot of noise competing for your attention. In private moments, you can quiet your mind and refill it with your positive imaginings.

Before each competition I wanted to win, I visualized that competition and the steps in front of me, all the way to the 1992 Olympic tryouts and eventually the World Games in 1994 in London, England, where I became the World Champion.

I recorded and listened to my goals and affirmations each night for three months until the night before the big Taekwondo competition in the World Games. I wanted to sleep on it, to fill my mind with visualized positive outcomes in sleep as in waking.

I got very specific with my visualizations: what I wanted to win, at what weight class, in what country, on what date. I pictured putting on my uniform, putting on my vest, so by the time I got to the weigh-ins and stepped into the ring, I had already done it thousands of times in my mind. I was already there. I had already won. I had already received my gold medal. I lived it, dreamed it, breathed it and eventually won it!

As Sun Tzu wrote: *"Victorious warriors win first and then go to war, while defeated warriors go to war first and then seek to win."*

If it worked for me, it can work for you. If you're reading this book, the desire is already there, so reinforce the desire and tune out the noise.

How many books have you read on business? On money? On self-help? How many audio lectures have you listened to? I have made a list of just some of these books and lectures that have made a difference to me, and included it in the bibliography in the back of this book. Study and master whatever you think might be relevant.

There really is a justification for a higher education—in this case, a higher *self*-education.

The difference between the wealthy entrepreneur and the middle- class wage slave is the power of setting goals with a time frame, and visualizing the whole thing already accomplished, over and over again until it is done.

Sun Tzu wrote: *"Opportunities multiply as they are seized."* Seizing oportunities requires confidence. When you visualize the goal accomplished, see what it looks like in your mind, and do this over and over again, you are developing a willingness to succeed and the confidence to seize the opportunities that present themselves. Success then breeds more success.

Feed the Good Wolf

The mind can only think one thought at a time, so changing the negative into a positive eliminates the negative.

Trained CPOs are always managing the actions of their own bodies and many others around them. This is how we "multitask": by taking action and managing action on several levels. This includes delegating action. When you delegate a task, you trust that individual to handle it, and turn your attention to the next challenge and focus on it fully.

I am coaching you to think like a specialist, the way a Certified Protection Operator does, but with a focus on moving your business forward in the wider Executive protection world.

Repeating positive affirmations (or, as Anthony Robbins says, *incantations*) feeds the good wolf. We are what we repeatedly do.

Excellence is not an isolated action, but a habit. Try to surround yourself with people who like to stay positive and upbeat. Pick them up when they stumble. Try to steer clear of habitually negative people who would rather feel sorry for themselves than do something effective about the situation.

If someone is wearing you down, find out if there's a positive lesson to be learned. Criticism you find upsetting may be intended constructively, but not always. Bad-intentioned people are in the minority, but they do exist. Those are the ones you can't change, satisfy, or make happy. If that's the case, keep them at arm's length (or farther).

If a trusted person is being negative, listen to what they have to say. I am a firm believer in always listening without making assumptions or interrupting. Then and only then can I respond with an intelligent answer and try to bring the subject back to where I want my thoughts and energy to be.

Try this when someone says something that is negative and draining: Ask them to repeat what they just said. Ask, "How can you reverse what you just said to work in your favor?" This takes the conversation back to where you want to be mentally. And perhaps both of you can learn from it and make a change to get you closer to your goal.

Keep in mind that both negative thoughts and positive thoughts are just thoughts. Negative thoughts have no power unless you keep dwelling on them and feeding the bad wolf. A gun has no power unless you fill the magazine, rack it and have the potential to pull the trigger. The same with your thoughts. They have no power unless you give them power. An unloaded gun virtually has no power, and the bad wolf has no power except what you give it.

Success breeds success, whereas negative energy will create a cavity in what should be your productive time. Try to fill the cavity with something important and healthy.

Be proactive on a daily basis. Read your goals aloud, clearly and convincingly. You can't afford to skip this one.

You can compare this to your relationship with your gun. After you shoot a gun, the next thing you do is clear it, make sure it's safe. Then you wash your hands. Then you clean your weapon.

Letting your mind dwell on an argument or bad experience is like failing to clean your weapon. Listening to people who don't believe in your success is like loading your weapon with faulty ammo or blanks.

Have a purpose. Choose a positive emotion to drive you. True emotion is something that touches your heart, something that moves and inspires you.

Anger will not propel you to success, but passion will.

The most reliable ammo for success is your own positive affirmations. Keep them handy.

Changing Habits

Just like we constantly go to the range to hone our skills with a firearm, you must constantly practice and train your mind so it becomes a habit. They say it takes 21 days to create a habit. So I will give you your first goal. For the next 21 days, write and read your goals daily. Be as specific as you can. The more detail, the more your mind will focus on what exactly it is you want.

You're developing the road map of your future. Your goals are the milestones.

This is where your imagination outshines the negative part of your mind, which can only dwell on the past. The future is yours to imagine, envision and create. Nobody else owns your future, and they can't throw up roadblocks to your imagination unless you agree.

Exercise Your Smile Muscles

We all know somebody who is bubbly, outgoing, positive no matter what. You may say to yourself, "Well, that's not me." In that case, I suggest you "fake it till you make it." A forced smile is still a smile, and it gets easier to smile the more you do it.

Smiling on the phone may sound silly, but believe it or not, you get feedback from your facial muscles that tells you you're happy.

Here is a challenge: Try "smiling from the inside." Smile from your eyes, and you will find your mouth can't resist turning up into a smile. You are tapping into these positive emotions which, when you think about it, are a gift to the people around you.

Don't be a mean mugger!

What Are Affirmations?

Affirmations are statements, proclamations, declarations and, basically, words that you repeat to yourself either in your mind or at the top of your lungs. You confirm or reaffirm to yourself and your subconscious mind what it is that you want to produce, the better life you want to bring about.

Get a recorder, a little notebook, and a book of positive affirmations. In your notebook write down the affirmations that inspire you the most. Try to add one of your own every day. Read from the book to your recorder, and play those back over and over, in the car or in bed.

If it is important to you, then it is worth writing down. Be as specific as possible and add as much detail as possible.

You also want to have a deadline to achieve your goals, so include your deadlines, both in your visualizations and your affirmations.

Positive affirmations really work, because *you shape the world around you according to what you believe.* You're not arguing with the negative voices, you're moving them out of your zone of focus by moving the positive to front and center.

For years I have read affirmations to help me achieve my goals. This has been across the board, whatever I was doing. I moved myself forward constantly with affirmations, whether in martial arts competition, with my magazine called *MMA Authority*, as a national speaker for my Kid Safe 911 Program, at my martial arts school of 20 years, or currently with my executive protection and security company.

If you want to be worth a million dollars, you need a million reasons to want it. You want a million reasons to help people. You want a million reasons to offer somebody service. If you're just sitting around wanting to be rich and wanting to be a millionaire, it will not happen. You must move yourself forward. You must motivate yourself. You do this by writing down your daily goals and working to achieve each goal by the end of the day. Always keep in mind your end result—how it will end.

Pushing forward and believing in yourself, having self-esteem, having high confidence, building a great team, having like-minded individuals around you, is what you really need to become successful. Build your mind with positive affirmations.

How or Why Do Affirmations Work?

It is like going to the gym and working out your muscles. It is like the muscle memory you develop when shooting a gun at the range. It works because now you are putting your mind through a workout. You are empowering your mind by repeatedly affirming (validating) what you want to create in your life or business. How many times have you talked yourself out of doing something for fear of the unknown, for fear of taking a risk or because of paralysis by over-analysis? Now let's reverse it. Start talking yourself into actually doing something. Instead of thinking fear, think *caution*; instead of risk, think *calculated risk*; instead of paralysis, just analyze and make your move.

You'd be surprised how often people forget that "make your move" step. Picture setting up a detail, doing your forward or advance, having your client's team in place, but then never driving to your destination. Won't happen, right? Same goes for business. Plan, prepare, and proceed. Taking a calculated risk means you know the challenges ahead and are prepared to meet them.

But you have to believe in yourself and one way to do this is by affirming you *can* do it and *will* achieve it by a certain time.

Your affirmations should be positive. Denying a negative is weak.

- *I will have a great day*. Not "I won't have a bad day."
- *I will make money*. Not "I won't lose money."
- *I will get this contract*. Not "I can't afford to lose this contract."
- *I will have a great interview*. Not "I won't have a bad interview."

Keep it simple and specific as to the exact thing you will attract or attain, including *when*. Repeat over and over so by the time you meet that client for that golden deal, you have already been there and done that in your mind hundreds of times.

Part of this is certainty that you can deliver a result. You've practiced until the motions come naturally. Affirmations alone don't work; they have to be supported by your training and experience in delivering a product clients will be happy to pay you for.

You have to believe in yourself and justify that belief. The competence has to be there first—a false certainty is as bad as a negative. A person who has never fired a gun won't hit the bullseye just by chanting, "I am going to hit the bullseye." The first loud concussion and recoil of the gun is going to completely shatter their world. And after they realize they missed—now what?

Repetition of the correct technique builds certainty of results. Repetition is the mother of all success—if done properly. Repeating the correct technique, the right wording—then you can mix in the affirmation factor.

Let's say you send two guys to the firing range who have performed the exact same number of repetitions. One of them clearly sees the bullet hitting the bullseye in his mind's eye; he knows he will attain that. The other guy simply takes aim and fires. Which one do you think will get more bullseyes?

Positive affirmation is a fundamental of achievement. I have seen many elite athletes do this and I have heard many famous speakers teach this.

Many successful sales people constantly affirm what they want:

- The numbers they will hit.
- The number of calls they will make.
- The bonus they will receive.
- The trip they'll win.

Basically, affirming what you want and repeating what you want can work in any part of your life: health, relationships, fitness, and in our case, good details for good executive protection clients.

Some of the best affirmations come from the spiritual philosophies underlying the martial arts. Here are two from www.zenthinking.net/blog/20-daily-morning-affirmations:

- I am a magnet of opportunity and will prosper doing only what I love.
- I am worthy of the abundance of life's blessings.

Flip the Negative to Positive

"Whatever the mind can believe and conceive, you can achieve." Napoleon Hill.

"We are what we repeatedly do. Excellence, then, is not an act, but a habit." Will Durant

Being successful in business and reaching the monetary goal that you set for yourself is a mindset that you can learn by practicing and training your mind. To make this happen, the rule to remember is: *What you focus on, you attract.*

Picture your mind as the laser on a gun. Where you point the gun is where the laser will go. Same with your thoughts. Train your mind, thoughts and actions to focus on what you want to attain in business and have a monetary reward attached to it.

Don't waste energy on thoughts about what you don't want. Anxiety, distress, and negative thinking lead to *paralysis by analysis.* You break out of it by taking effective action, training, working out. There are a lot of ways to do this, and all of them involve *action.*

Analysis paralysis can shut down any forward progress toward attaining your goal or goals. This is extremely counterproductive and depletes positive energy and thoughts. That is how negative energy and thinking block future goals from being attained.

Most likely, if you are constantly thinking and dwelling on negative energy, you are getting negative reinforcement from people around you. This is the exact opposite of a positive affirmation and produces the opposite result. Take a break from those influences if you need to.

An easy way to displace negative thinking is to write down your goals and read them each day. If you need to add, edit or delete some of your goals (which are your thoughts), then do so.

We all have challenges in daily life that compete with positive thoughts for our attention. It wouldn't be realistic to say you must *stay* positive. I'm asking you to *repeat* the positive to yourself whenever you need to, to push negative thoughts out of the way.

Maybe there's somebody in your life who is easily overwhelmed by life's challenges. Work with that person to meet those challenges. Meet negative with positive as you can. If that's not well received, if the person seems intent on tearing you down—or agrees with those who do—that's not your ideal relationship.

No human can ever stop negative energy. A better approach is to treat negative energy the way a martial artist treats the incoming thrust of his opponent. It's energy, isn't it? So flip it around, use it to reinforce your forward momentum.

In the EP world we have to constantly plan for the things that can go wrong. We visualize all the scenarios. Don't confuse this with negative visualization. You're not turning your thoughts inward and dwelling on personal shortcomings or faults. You're visualizing several steps ahead, the various moves and counter-moves to keep the advantage on the known or unknown opponent.

Many times, situations just snap into our thoughts. As a CPO, you channel that energy into your advance or forward to make sure what *can* go wrong *doesn't*. You just turned a potential negative situation with negative thoughts into a positive plan for your detail. This works the same with attaining your goal, changing a negative thought into a positive one.

We live in a world where negativity sells. Newspaper reporters look for the graphic, the gruesome, the gory—basically the opposite of your ideal scene of "everything running smoothly." If there is a problem, a negative reporter will worry at the problem until it becomes a story.

Ten people will love a restaurant and mention it to a couple of friends. One person will hate it and tell the world. If something positive is said about you, it's up to you to make sure the world knows it. (This is a good use for your Facebook business page. You will create your positive image with your marketing.)

If you're going to sell a product on Amazon, you need to get a ton of positive reviews in a hurry, preferably right at the time of launch. Why? Because without those positive reviews, one or two complainers can sink you in the product rankings—maybe for good. Some people delight in poisoning "public opinion" about you. Don't sink to their level of unhappiness. The only effective counterattack for negative statements is to create in greater abundance with good works on a much broader scale.

When it comes to your own sense of self-worth, give yourself a positive review.

Being Positive Is a habit

If you have negative chatter going on in your head, then arguing back and getting mad or antagonistic won't do it. Just stop for a moment and listen to those negative voices. Who's talking trash? Do you recognize some favorite phrases? Do you know someone who used to tear you down using similar phrases—a parent, coach, maybe a drill instructor?

If you can identify one or two of these negative voices, you can begin to separate out your own mental voice—the one that practices those positive affirmations I suggested. "I'm the best at what I do. My clients have total confidence in me because I've earned it. I am the leader in my field in my community."

Being positive is a habit you learn by repeating your affirmations. Fill your mind with them and you will shove all the negativity right out of your space.

You have to step away from people who are not being positive. If you can do this and have a team of people who stop placing the blame on others, your company will grow.

Blaming others is also a habit, and a dangerous one. This is very true in today's fast-paced social media world. What I'm getting at here is that blaming others is complete bullshit.

Blaming others is a way of dodging responsibility for the way things have turned out. *You can't solve a problem without owning it.* If you insist on saying it's someone else's problem, it will never get solved.

Reacting Versus Responding

The reality you create for yourself is entirely dependent on how you choose to live, how you react or respond to conditions within and around you.

To react is to let a reflex take over. To respond is to make a considered decision, even if it's lightning-fast. If you do something you'll regret later, that is probably a reaction, though it may also be an uninformed decision.

Do a thought exercise here. Right now, take a moment to make up some examples of reacting to a situation, and some examples of responding to a situation.

Outwitting Negativity with Goals

If your goals are written down, you can return to them and get above the negativity of others. Goals put your attention out into the future, which is yours to create. If you look far enough ahead, there's nothing out there to stand in the way of your goals. *Obstacles are always smaller in comparison to a big enough goal.*

When you work out, be fully in the moment. Allow the body to recharge and circulate that energy. Try to empty your mind, or repeat your affirmations. Don't put energy into thinking about the bills you have to pay or an argument you had. Yes, those things exist too. Stay in the moment—physical effort makes this easier to do.

Well trained and experienced CPOs tune out the internal chatter and focus on what's around them.

To maximize potentiality, you must get out of your own way. The task in front of you is all that matters. In moments of extreme urgency, you take the direct path because you have to. To carry this ability over into day-to-day living requires some creativity. With goals, and with daily and weekly targets that add up to goal attainment, you add some necessity to each moment.

Fear is a close companion to negativity. Fear will create barriers that only you and your positive energy can break down. For example, you decide you want to stimulate your lymphatic and cardiovascular system, so you decide to go for a run on the beach. While you are running, you are thinking about this problem or that issue, what will happen later, etc. You may blur reality because of what has happened to you in the past or what you think might happen to you in the future. Your mind mistakes the negative thought for reality and builds on that instead of the goals you've envisioned.

In your mind, you play movies of how things are, how they could be, how they should be, how they will be, and "how it ends." Don't forget that you were the one who created that movie in the first place, and that you wrote the whole script yourself.

The power of mind and its ability to manifest its own reality is a two-edged sword. You can manifest your goals or your problems. Stick to the goals.

Creating a Positive Environment

When you're working with a team, create an environment for the team to keep everyone working toward a common objective. Encourage the mentality that, as a unit, they can overcome anything.

Creating an environment that allows people to think freely while maintaining and charting the course of a detail or a business endeavor is very important. It's very important to always have an environment where people can freely talk to each other without imposing their will onto you. You want to have a comfortable environment where people can set goals, raise the bar, and reach for the stars without ever being dethroned by someone's negative thoughts, by someone always saying that it can't be done. If there is somebody around you who constantly cannot work with other people, my advice is: Fire them.

Be positive even when you don't feel that way at first. You can pull yourself out of the doldrums any time by the simple exercise of saying something positive and taking positive action toward an established goal.

You may have heard people say that "what will be will be," that we are what the environment makes us. I say no. The environment is what we make it, by shaping people's perceptions as well as by our physical actions. Master manifestors understand this so well that it seems instinctive. Don't be deceived. *Positivity is a drill like batting practice, or working out. The successful guys are the ones who have put in their reps.*

Treat each negative thought like a passer-by who wants to stop and chat while you're on a detail. They have nothing to offer except noise. I'm not saying you can or should suppress all stray thoughts. "What's for lunch?" is fine. "What's wrong with me?" is a sinkhole. Don't step in it.

Negative thinking, fatalistic thinking, limited thinking, are very effective at keeping you a small-time operator. Entertain the big ideas, the positive thoughts, and leave negativity to the losers. Be so sure of yourself that you radiate confidence.

The only value of past failures is to assess how you'll handle it differently next time. File that information and discard the emotional content. Stay within your positive mindset and create those positive thoughts, skip the negative, and cultivate the joy of solving problems creatively.

Choose Who You're With

I have briefly touched on this already, but want to bring it fully into focus. You need to choose who you're with in business the same way you would choose who you would be with in a war. It's that simple.

Your actions come from your thoughts and beliefs about everything: about people, things, professions, values, manners, and life.

This is exactly why you want to have like-minded individuals working with you. There are so many different things about people: their values, their manners, their background, their culture. Everything eventually ties back into these two things: what is the main objective of your company, and what is the main moral compass of your company? Are you all on the same page? Do you have such differences in viewpoint about life and lifestyles that it might impede your success in running a company?

Pick the best people to do the best jobs, and move forward. But move forward in a direction that you believe in, not in a direction that you do not believe in.

If you don't believe in the direction that you're going, you will not get there. Something will happen along the way to derail you. Most probably it will be you who derails yourself, because you are not following your purpose. It is your own thoughts that derail you the most.

I try to surround myself with people who:

1) can make me better by sharing what they know,
2) believe in me and embrace my goals,
3) are good "team players" and help the team.

At the same time, I work hard to be that kind of person for those around me.

There will always be people who need and deserve your support. You may or may not be the primary breadwinner for a family. If you are the sole support, the runway to success is going to be longer, because there is a certain amount of income you have to keep bringing home no matter what. In the beginning, you'll be working for somebody else 30 or 40 hours a week, and then working for yourself another 50. Those are the grim facts.

If you're lucky enough to have a two-income family, all this will go a lot smoother and faster. If your spouse is willing to help you and support you, this is crucial. You have to have somebody who is lifting you up and not putting you down—someone you can trust. If you have somebody who's putting you down and not picking up the slack, it will be a long, arduous road. Do not make this mistake. There have been times in business that I have declined to become partners, especially on paper, with someone who I may have trusted, but there was too much unpredictability with their spouses.

Make sure the people in your life are able to contribute to you in some meaningful way and get recognition for it. People love to help; they get upset when they don't have a way to give back. This is true for your children as well. Teach them that their help is welcome and valuable. It is up to you to understand that their help may be at a very primitive stage. They need successes helping at their level, just as you need successes helping at your level.

I've often said, "Surround yourself with positive people." This is especially important when you're hiring. One jerk can drag the team down. I don't care if he's a superstar bodyguard. A bad attitude isn't hard to spot during the interview process, and you can include questions designed to detect it.

Outside of work, I try to steer clear of people who always have to have drama in their lives. A woman who is being stalked by an ex-boyfriend is great for a client, but maybe not so great as a girlfriend.

Giving this kind of personal advice is tricky. There's no way I can know your exact situation. I can't stop you from taking on a "project," and maybe I shouldn't try. But remember that *you don't have to*. You can always keep looking. A matchmaking website is probably a better place to find romance than a bar.

Having a spoiler in your group, having somebody that undermines your opinion, having somebody in your company who is leaning toward the opposite side of what you're dreaming, makes no sense. In the end, it will act like a cavity in a tooth. If it doesn't get fixed, the whole tooth will become rotten. The same thing can happen to your business.

I have no time in my life for people who continuously try to elevate themselves above others in the team or the company, who continuously promote that they are so much better than everyone else, and that no one else can do their job.

In the end, their job can be replaced and will be replaced if they do not follow and play by the rules. It's not always one person who makes the rules. It's a group of people who come together and say, "This is the best thing for our company," whether it's one person with two other people, or one person and a partner, or a board of people. The goal is to move the company in a good direction, a healthy direction, maintain old customers, keep new customers, and keep your staff happy. These are the things that are important to being successful.

It's very important to keep people around you who inspire you as well, not just you inspiring them. Everybody on the team has to be a cheerleader for the team, and accept people on the team as they are, so that it benefits everybody. Not one person can single-handedly run a company successfully and with great efficiency. It has to be done with a team of people that are like-minded. In some cases, you bring in people who are not like-minded to discuss ideas and brainstorm to find a better solution. However, if someone is actively running your company and helping you, make sure that they have the endgame in mind, not just what they want in the beginning.

We live in an instant-gratification and fast-food environment. We all want it right now. With money, you can't have it right now. You have to wait and earn it. And if you can't earn it, then don't begrudge others who have it. I've never worked for a poor person; have you? When people see money, it sometimes changes the fabric of their being. I have seen it over and over again. Usually the people who are changed by money are stubborn and self-promoting. They are also known as victims.

I choose to not work with victims. I choose to work with survivors and winners. People who are constantly talking about being a victim of society, race, color, creed, ethnicity: that doesn't work out for me. Likewise, if they have a very, very strong opinion which they must promote such as being anti-guns, or anti-men, we can't work with them.

6

Creating Your Future With Goals

First of all, you have to develop a burning desire to succeed. Do you really want this? If you do, you are going to read everything on the subject, anything relevant, reach or watch or consult anyone who has valuable experience. There are no shortcuts to success. It is hard work. It is educating yourself—and I'm not talking about organized education like college.

If you want to be an expert in this field, then you have to go out and experience it. You have to become a person who is a sponge to everything that you can get your hands on in order to overcome any objections you have in your own mind. You have to be willing to separate yourself from the everyday Joe or Jill who lives a "fast-food" life where they just want their burger.

I have coached many people in executive protection, and helped many of them start a business. The ones who succeed are the ones who can generate their own drive, who can get excited about their own ideas and convey that excitement to someone else. If there's nothing happening, they make something happen. They can confront an empty appointment calendar and get pumped up about filling that calendar.

The Concept of Urgency

I have found that you are more capable than you often realize, but you have to find what is going to push you. You can do things greater than you thought possible if something important is at stake.

We see examples of people performing nearly impossible physical feats when they are driven by necessity. I once asked someone if she could swim across a wide channel in the Intercoastal Waterway. She hesitated at first, but said yes. But when I asked if she could do it in four minutes, she laughed and said no. I took it one step further and asked if she could do it if one of her kids was drowning on the other side. That changed everything. Once you find that internal motivation, nearly anything is possible. If her child's life was on the line, nothing would stop her.

Can you muster that sense of urgency about your day-to-day business activities? That's kind of a reach, I know, but try it. Think of who depends on you and what they need, and get the idea of fulfilling those needs. Do this exercise whenever you need motivation.

Developing a sense of urgency is very important. As I said before:

Whatever can be done today, do it now.

Whatever can be done tomorrow, do it today.

When I had the martial arts school, when parents couldn't come to me to sign the paperwork, I would go to them, to their homes, to their offices. I would make it work. I was hustling. I have always maintained a sense of urgency to meet my goals, to take care of business first. If I was going out, I would hand out business cards. I wasn't going to wait for them to call me. I would say, "Give me your number and I'll call you to set up the appointment."

You have to keep rediscovering the urgency of making your goals, whatever they may be. It may be small goals at first: to get out of a financial hole, to get just a little bit ahead, and then to get more ahead. It might be to get yourself "out of the gutter," whatever that means to you. It might be to get your mind above ground, thinking forward, projecting a future.

Start making decisions now. You have to make decisions on a daily basis to make sure that you're on top of the game. If you don't make a decision, that is a decision. If you're not making proactive decisions, then you're going to be making reactive decisions. Be proactive.

Keep in mind that at some point, you may have to reinvent your company to keep yourself motivated and keep yourself on top of the game.

It's like you're running a race. If you feel the hot breath of a competitor on your neck, that's when you discover your overdrive mode. If you can't feel that when you're all by yourself in your little office in the garage or in a corner of the kitchen, staring at the phone, you have to invent a way to make yourself feel it. If you find yourself wandering into the kitchen, opening the fridge, deciding there's nothing you want for the thousandth time, picture that competitor breathing down your neck, exploiting your moment of weakness, and don't let him do it.

Many people are incapable of performing at a certain level, due to limitations beyond their control. Those who aren't so limited have no business accepting a handicap, no excuse to fail. We should push ourselves to attain our highest possible level of achievement and not settle for less. Do it for all of those who can't.

Be Passionate About What You Do

If you don't have fun doing something, you're going to lose your passion for it. If you lose your passion for it, then that's it. It's a car without any gasoline.

I was driven to have enough money so I could always help my mom, my dad, and my brother. If I had children, I'd want to give them a head start to become great at whatever their passion might be, and meanwhile provide them with healthy food and healthy choices.

People say money is not the most important thing in life. Maybe not, but money touches the most important things in your life. I'm not chasing money; I'm chasing what money can do.

Money is a very powerful tool. It can be used for good, and it can be used for evil. If you take your money and use it to empower your children and other people and you've done a lot of good with it, you just doubled the value of your money.

It's going to come back to you, in buckets, because other people will believe in you and know that your success is their success.

Goal Setting

In the previous chapter, we looked at how you can defeat negativity by putting your attention on the future. You do that by setting goals.

The difference between ordinary and extraordinary is that little word *extra*. Are you willing to make the time and effort to write down your goals, affirm your goals and create a burning desire to attain them?

Without a goal there is no glory. Write down a goal and read it. Assign a target date to accomplish that goal. Set the bar high enough that there's some glory in the achievement. And then drive for the goal.

Writing down goals is one of the easiest things you can do. It is the first step toward goal attainment. You won't attain a goal that you haven't named and envisioned.

A study done by Harvard University in 1979 showed why 3% of Harvard MBAs were earning ten times as much as the other 97% combined.

My question to you is the same question asked of the Harvard MBA graduates.

"Have you set clear, written goals for your future and made plans to accomplish them?"

- 84% had no specific goals at all.
- 13% had goals, but they were not committed to paper.
- 3% had clear, written goals and plans to accomplish them.

In 1989, the interviewers again interviewed the graduates of that class. Results?

The 13% of the class who had goals were earning, on average, twice as much as the 84% who had no goals. The three percent who had clear written goals were earning, on average, ten times as much as the other

97% put together. For this and other great inspirations, read *What They Don't Teach You at Harvard Business School: Notes from a Street-smart Executive*, by Mark H. McCormack.

How come so many people don't set goals or don't write them down? Maybe they try it briefly and give up too soon. Repetition will get you there, so don't bail out along the way.

In describing his "Management by Objectives" approach, Peter Drucker offered this handy way to remember what your goals should be like: make them SMART.

- Specific
- Measurable
- Acceptable
- Realistic
- Time-bound

There are several variations of what SMART stands for. You can Google them if you're curious. I like Drucker's version best, because each point is grounded in reality, and all of them are important.

Specific. Are you going to "land five new clients this month," or "talk to a bunch of people"? Make a goal as specific as you can. It may change as you gain more experience. But you need something that will give you a clear mental picture you can hold firmly in mind.

Measurable. If a goal is measurable, you'll know when you've attained it. And if you do attain it, I don't care if it was *motivational* or not (that's one of the "M" variations). It moved you forward.

Acceptable. Acceptable means the team will buy into it. That's important, right? I'm not saying it has to be as popular as free money. What I'm saying is that if you get a lot of push-back instead of buy-in, it was either not well thought out or not well communicated.

Realistic. Make your goals realistic. Otherwise you set yourself up to fail in your own eyes. "I will land five celebrities as clients" would be unrealistic for most people starting out in the business. "I will obtain five good celebrity leads" is something you can probably do. And if you've set a goal that is acceptable to your team, then it's realistic to expect their cooperation.

Time-bound. This is perhaps the most important "SMART" feature. If a goal will take years to attain, include it in your ten-year plan, but not in your plan for the first six months.

Consider what it is you want and then commit to it.

Executive protection is a tough industry to conquer. Without goal setting that is both visionary and realistic, it can seem impossible to get ahead.

Take a look at your personal income. What is the best year you've ever had? What were you doing that enabled you to reach that level?

Here's another calculation that is going to take some real work: what does the **gross** income (revenue) of your business have to be, in order to **net** the amount you just stated?

The 7 Ps

The 7 Ps is a military saying that I have found extremely useful. There are variants of this, but the one I like the best is: Proper Prior Planning Prevents Piss-Poor Performance. Planning is an essential part of being successful. It is the roadmap to help get you from where you are to your end goal, with milestones along the way. Though your plan may change a dozen times to deal with changing circumstances or new opportunities, it keeps you on track toward your ultimate goal. Without a plan, you're not choosing the best possible route. You can't just keep putting one foot in front of the other and hope to get anywhere.

Targeting Yourself for Achievement

A target is something to shoot for. Simple, right? If I put a gun in your hand right now, point out a target such as a paper bullseye or silhouette, a clay pigeon, or a metal spinner, and tell you to shoot, assuming you are trained in firearms, I know you're comfortable with the motions. I know you can hit that target, still or moving, with a fair degree of competence.

Okay, let's change it up a little bit. I say "shoot" without telling you what to shoot at. What do you do? You stop and ask questions. You can't shoot without knowing what your target is, unless you're just firing off rounds into the air.

In business, when I say you should pick your targets, I'm talking about milestones toward attainment of your overall goals. This can be as small as a to-do list for the day, or as large as a ten-year plan.

A to-do list is a good start, but there may be a tendency to only think about the things you are "supposed to do." Just as important is to keep those visionary goals or longer-term targets in view. Those are the things nobody is bugging you about, because it's your vision, not theirs.

I recommend that you always have a written program with six or eight steps that will move you closer to one of your short-term goals.

You can have several programs going: a program to generate leads through postcards and Internet marketing, a program to build up a full team, and another one to organize your contacts. And keep in mind keeping them simple.

You also want to keep your clients happy and smiling. Customer service plays a huge role in keeping clients happy.

The movie *Groundhog Day* is a fantasy where one guy keeps reliving the same day. Isn't that all of us, to some degree? Many people feel as if they do all this work and never move the ball more than a few yards. They are stuck; they are in a holding pattern, but for how long?

In the movie, the Bill Murray character did everything he could think of to escape the rut. He found out the hard way that bailing out of life isn't an option. What finally did work for him was to learn a lesson from everything that didn't go his way, and take a fresh approach the next time. Life always gives us that opportunity, if we are paying attention.

How long until *you* realize your growth is being held back by doing things the same old way?

I said in the introduction to this book that business is like a tree. It is the same with your life: if it is not growing, it is dying. Healthy growth means progress in a worthwhile direction.

A tree has a built-in blueprint. If you're taking over Dad's business, you have a blueprint (though probably not expressed on paper in as much detail as you'd like) and you need to study it thoroughly before introducing any changes.

What I'm trying to give you here is a more general pattern based on my own experience in the business. That pattern will give you a good starting point for drawing your own blueprint for your unique set of circumstances.

An architect uses blueprints to ultimately have a finished product in front of him before they dig the first hole. Your business should run similar to that. A blueprint on paper that you have created in your mind should direct your company in the direction that will achieve positive cash flow. Without this blueprint, it's going to be a long struggle.

An architect has to visualize the final result and get this picture firmly in mind before drawing up the detailed plans. It's going to start with a series of preliminary sketches, with input from the client (in the case of your business, this might be a partner or investor).

Your statement of long-term goals is like a preliminary sketch. Commit it to paper, consult it frequently and let your vision evolve as you learn more about the business and your personal and family needs.

Where do you want to be in ten or fifteen years? What kind of home will you be living in? Where will your children be going to school? How much money do you need to sock away in order to enjoy a comfortable retirement with your family and continue to support their needs?

As I have said many times, money is not the most important thing in life, but it touches the most important things in our lives. By setting clear, specific, time-bound goals you can now measure your achievements and see forward progress. This will help clear the air of any confusion so you can find a clear path to success and attain your SMART goals.

In setting goals, it is important to start with a "big picture" and then work backwards. With that "big picture" in mind as your destination, set achievable goals that move you forward within stated time frames. Have a three-month plan, a six-month plan, one, two, and five-year plans. Write these down and hold yourself accountable. After you have set a five- or ten-year plan, work backwards. Make a plan for the next year, the next six months, three months, and so on, down to the coming week.

Setting short-term goals allows you to see your results quicker and keeps you on the path or correct course. Without short-term measured goals, it would be very easy to get distracted and drift off course.

Set a date when you're going to pull in that first protection detail. By that date, you have to have one client. I don't care if they give you 50 bucks to do an all-day event—you got your first client. Let's hit another goal: maybe get another client who is willing to pay 75 dollars. Then you set the next goal and keep going. That's how you start.

Setting lifetime goals should be a fun activity. You can say anything you want to, change it as often as you want to. Whatever positive outcomes you can envision will go on the list. It helps to have role models, real world examples of how successful you can be.

Reward Yourself

When you arrive at a milestone that you've been working on for weeks, or maybe years, that's a time for celebration.

If you're like me, you don't like grandstanders. Some of these end zone celebrations are so over the top that you think the guy must spend as much time rehearsing for his celebrations as he does learning the playbook.

That's not my style, and it's not keeping the low profile I advised you about in *The Bodyguard Myth*.

But you're entitled to take a win. Basically if the goal is worth achieving it is worth celebrating. You earned that pat on the back, and you should accept it.

Acknowledging this or any achievement raises self-confidence. When people are confident, they always seem to have the wind at their backs, sending them in the right direction. Confidence is one of the hardest things to engender in someone. But once they are confident, not much can stop their determination.

All of this is attainable if you have established your goals and are working toward them. But don't just *reward* yourself: *invest* in yourself. Make your money grow and eventually work for you. In the beginning, you work to make money. In the end, you should let your money work hard for you.

Once you hit a goal, you are now in a position to move to the next goal. In the early stages of your business, that may be the moment when you let go of your day job, or that you have the number of steady clients needed to put you "in the black." As you keep moving forward, these target attainments may go from buying your first house (if that is where you want to invest) to setting a new monthly billing record, or even to hitting another level of the million-dollar club.

Always keep things in perspective. Don't get frustrated if the goal still seems far off. Every small victory is a step toward the greater goal. Sometimes you hit a home run, but don't assume you've suddenly broken through to a new level. The game hasn't fundamentally changed. If it's not broken, don't fix it.

If you don't achieve the goal that you set, go back to your "to do" list and see what mark you didn't hit.

How are you reaching your customers? When you contact a potential customer, how do you convert that to a sale? How do you perform your job, once you have it? How do you maintain your client base? It is a whole package of behaviors that you are tweaking until you get the results you want.

Dedication to Your Goals

If you are truly dedicated to your goals, then you will cut out the things and people who don't bring you closer to that goal.

I will step away from anyone who becomes a distraction to my goals, particularly if they want me to think small, or think less of myself, or are holding me to some past failure. I still want to help those people, but I don't want their business advice.

Striving toward my goals has put me in front of some of the smartest attorneys, CEOs, millionaire and billionaire handlers. I learned from each and every one of them, and I'm thankful for those lessons. But I learned! How they talked, what their hobbies were, what their family structure was, what books they read, what clubs they were involved with, and what other goals they, themselves, were working on.

I always entertain conversations about business, no matter how big or small the deal, but when it comes to small talk, current events, or personal drama, I lose interest quickly. I want to speak with people about ideas!

7

Setting Up Your Business

Success will never come without some risks, but the know-how to succeed in this business is something I have developed and honed over many years, and I'm happy to share it with you.

Many in this industry do not hone their business skills, and don't make it in the big leagues. Yes, they can wing it and do some executive protection here or there, but they haven't studied and mastered sound business practices.

Let's put a blueprint—a basic foundation—there for you to build on. Use this as a starting point. But your business will be uniquely yours, and remember: only you can make it work.

Location, Location, Location

Where will my business be located? Demographics are a huge key to success. As you create your business locally, cultivate your contacts in other metropolitan areas. As you grow, get tentacles in the business as far out as you can. Get familiar with the rates that are charged in different areas. Generally, the larger the city, the more you can charge.

Initial Expenditures

What Is My Capital Investment?

Your business income will eventually have to cover overhead, rent, and staff. You will need to hire people to take care of your taxes and your bills so you don't have to worry about it.

If you are going to self-fund and not seek loans, which is what I recommend, your main investment is going to be your spare time, after turning in a competent day's work at your day job.

You can't quit your day job until the business income is enough to replace the income you already make, and until you know the business income will be sustained.

Executive protection details have to be profitable from the start. In the beginning you will do most of the work. You're going to have to hustle. Set your goals, write a plan out, work the plan.

I've never borrowed money to start a business. As a firm believer in multiple streams of income, I've borrowed money from banks to do big real estate deals. However, when you are starting out a business, debt can interfere with expansion and flexibility in a very major way.

Setting Up Your Office

You need your computer, your phone, your contact list, and your website. I can help get you set up with a website that is already generating traffic. If your geographic area is open, you can get a great head start.

A printer is indispensable. They are cheap—it is the ink that can get expensive. You no doubt have a weapon and a license to use it. A Kevlar vest will come in handy. Your contractors will bring their own gear.

You'll need software to manage your calendar, email, and contacts. Google Apps is free or very cheap, and is good enough for some very large organizations. If you already have Outlook, that's fine too. Whether you take notes on all your business conversations in a plain notebook or an elaborate organizer makes no difference, just as long as you consistently take notes and preserve them in a way that will be easily accessible. It is essential that you have and demonstrate a very good grasp of what you have discussed with your potential clients or current clients. That in itself communicates a level of organization and competence that will give your clients confidence, not to mention make your life so much easier.

Don't rent an office until you know it will pay for itself by facilitating new business. At that point, the additional business it generates will more than offset the cost. The main thing you need office space for is face-to-face interviews. But it is a luxury, not a necessity, for a startup EP agency. I've had my own office for a long time, but I've found that not many of my interviews are conducted there. If the prospect is across the bay in Tampa, I'll more likely go see him. If he's a couple of hours away in Orlando, we'll do the deal on the phone. So it's not that great a handicap to be home-based.

Your most valuable asset will be your contact database. You'll have vendor contacts, customer contacts, and contractor (bodyguard) contacts. Keep them in three separate files. If you're not a wiz at this sort of thing, find somebody who is.

Marketing and Promotion

One more expenditure is absolutely vital, and that is marketing. You need a social media presence—minimally Facebook and LinkedIn. A website that generates leads can double the speed of your ramp-up to profitability. But you have to take the steps to get your website to appear on the first couple of pages of your category with search engine optimization (SEO). Getting a logo and a basic website designed will pay off far more than it costs.

The unpredictability of a paycheck is tough at first, but if you never stop marketing, never stop promoting yourself and working your connections, the big payoff will come. Some get spoiled after doing a few high-paying EP jobs. Now all of a sudden, they won't work for less than $400 per day. That's OK as long as it works for you.

If you follow my advice on marketing, you will develop "brand recognition"—a reputation for ethical, competent work, and for being able to field a great team on short notice. Again, connections are king, so it pays to reward those who gave you a boost, when the roles are reversed.

I will go into much more detail about marketing in a later chapter.

Staffing

At this point in my business, I have an office manager/client services director who helps populate and schedule my details. Everything for staffing runs through that person, while I concentrate on the contracts. The team members of my details are all subcontractors.

The Subcontracting Network

Hiring Yourself Out as an Individual

You will probably do several details as a subcontractor or "hired hand" on a team before you start getting steady work directly from clients. Use this experience wisely.

Too many Certified Protection Operators think like specialists only, with no understanding of business and how fast it can go south because you said the wrong thing at the wrong time. Take advantage of every opportunity to observe a good team lead at work: how he interacts, speaks, negotiates deals, and manages a team. This is critical in many ways.

Before your phone rings for the first time, you should have an idea of what sort of clients you can help effectively, and which ones you'd like to help, and you can gain this knowledge as a subcontractor.

Subcontracting Others

The one thing you don't want to do is turn down viable work due to your own scheduling limitations. From the start, network with colleagues so you can accept details you can't personally handle because of your day job or other scheduling conflicts.

If you get a lead that you can't personally deliver, you need reliable subcontractors so you don't have to turn down work. Breaking even on a job because you outsourced it, and ending up with another happy client, is progress. Wasting a hard-won lead by turning down the work because you're already booked is a step backward.

Setting up your own business looks like a gamble. You're going to hear discouraging statistics about the high failure rate of new businesses.

Maybe you know somebody who failed at one of these start-ups. It's usually because of some common and very avoidable error. It's very common for a skilled craftsman to think of himself as a businessman because he can do a great job and make a client happy. It's true that you need to be able to deliver a great product, but the real test is whether you can deliver that same result by sending someone else to do it, and manage the detail remotely.

Subcontracting A Detail From Your Company

Other executive protection companies can be a good source of business. Maybe a company out-of-state needs someone with your local knowledge, on-the-ground familiarity and connections. Or a local agency needs added manpower on a short-term basis.

Be a good sub; don't try to be the boss. Accept whatever duties and responsibilities are assigned to you and carry them out well. Ask for more business—from the contractor, not the client.

These guidelines will keep you out of trouble when working under another firm:

- Follow instructions precisely.
- Don't act like a big shot or try to enforce"your way" of doing things.
- Don't start managing schedules. If I'm the overall contractor and an internal team starts to change internal scheduling without coordinating with me or my client, it will impede my ability to run things at 100% effectiveness.
- Get the information you need to carry out your duties, but respect the "need-to-know" boundaries.
- Learn and respect the chain of command.
- Do a great job.
- Make friends and continue to build those relationships.
- Never steal a client. In a small industry like ours, it's a business-killer. If a client approaches you to work directly for them, report this immediately.

Lenny Bogdanos

Outside Consultants

How soon do you need professional help to get your financial books set up properly? You need to have fully standard bookkeeping in place before your first tax filing, and probably much sooner. It's a challenge to track your money when it comes in at irregular intervals. It's all too easy to overdraw your checking account, because your online balance won't show you the checks that haven't cleared.

Bookkeeper

A bookkeeper can do a lot more for you than keep the checkbook balanced. At tax time, they'll make a package for your tax accountant of everything that needs to be reported. In the meantime, they can show you reports of your cash flow and other indicators of your agency's financial health.

In the early days, it may be enough to throw your receipts in a shoebox and have your bookkeeper record them once a month. Make sure you've got receipts for every purchase and a photocopy of every check you write and every check you deposit.

A bookkeeper's job is literally to keep up your books (your financial records). Your bookkeeper records your day-to-day transactions and makes sure you have the same amount of money the bank says you have, plus any income the bank doesn't know about yet, minus any spending the bank doesn't know about yet. The bookkeeper keeps your bank accounts balanced.

Your bookkeeper will also do your billing. They will create an invoice every time somebody owes you money, and send out the bill, as well as monthly statements—reminders of what was initially billed, what has been paid, and what is still owed.

Billings must go out on time, or you're operating a charity instead of a business.

Certified Public Accountant (CPA)

A certified public accountant (CPA) has a higher level of education. They do these highly skilled things:

1) establish a system for the bookkeeper to use,
2) prepare your tax filing documents.

An accountant can do bookkeeping, of course, but their hourly rate is two to five times as high, so I wouldn't bring in a CPA for things your bookkeeper (or you yourself) can do easily in QuickBooks or the like.

Generally speaking, government agencies want one thing from businesses: tax money. Licenses and permits are basically taxes, as well as ways to set standards. If you don't get all the licenses and permits required by law, those agencies won't get their slice of your pie. Your accountant will "make you legal" and set up the income and expense categories so you aren't paying more taxes than you have to. They will:

- Set up your "books" (accounting records).
- Ensure that you give the various agencies their legal due.
- Dish them up a sliver of your pie instead of a big slice.
- Represent you in any negotiations with the IRS or other agencies.

Your CPA can do all the above. An enrolled agent, or EA, is equally recognized by the IRS when it comes to tax matters, but an EA who isn't also a CPA is probably not the best choice to set up your initial books.

A bookkeeper's hourly rate is much lower than an accountant's: $25-50 rather than $125-200. A good bookkeeper won't overstep their bounds and give you tax advice. If you find a bookkeeper you trust, they probably refer all their clients to a particular CPA to set up the books and prepare the tax returns.

Setting up Business Accounts

Once you have a business checking account established, get a CPA to set up QuickBooks or some other accounting software for you and create the various income accounts, expense accounts, and other "buckets" each transaction will go into. This helps to make your business tax filing as simple as possible later.

You can get a bit of QuickBooks help from https://community.intuit.com. Types of accounts you might set up:

- Assets
- Liabilities
- Capital/Equity
- Income or Revenue
- Cost of Goods Sold
- Expenses or Overhead Costs
- Other Income
- Other Expense

Your Chart of Accounts might look something like that, at the top level. You can think of these as file folders in a cabinet, all of them empty until you make some money or spend some money or save some money. Your accountant will probably set up your accounts using account numbers, because it makes it easy for them to categorize each transaction without giving it too much thought, similar to this:

1000 - 1999 Assets (each Asset account would be assigned a number between 1000 and 1999)

2000 - 2999 Liabilities

3000 - 3999 Equity

4000 - 4999 Income or Revenue

5000 - 5999 Job Costs/Cost of Goods Sold

6000 - 6999 Overhead Costs or Expenses

7000 - 7999 Other Income

8000 - 8999 Other Expense

Your accountant can't keep you legal if you're not. But assuming you are operating within the rules, your accountant can put each transaction in the bucket that gives you the best tax advantage. The object of this game is to offset as much income with business expenses as possible.

Determine Your Business Legal Structure

Flying under the radar of government agencies, ignoring the laws until you're big enough to get noticed, can influence you to stay small. And it can really backfire when you do get noticed. The government can come after you for back taxes, fines and penalties, and might even padlock your business, simply for operating without the necessary paperwork. Your paper trail needs to support the case you're making with the IRS or other agencies.

As you set up your business, you will discover that there is a lot to know regarding the legal structure of your business, understanding regulations, permits and rules that have been set up to maintain high standards. Some of these requirements get pretty specific, such as the minimum amount of space to be provided per staff member, fire safety arrangements, lighting levels, ventilation and temperature control.

It may be very much to your advantage to find a mentor in the nonprofit federal agency called SCORE (Service Corps of Retired Executives) to help you understand and sort all this out. SCORE is a nationwide resource partner with the U.S. Small Business Administration (SBA), which is a federal agency providing free or almost-free support to small businesses and entrepreneurs. There are over 300 SCORE chapters, and they have many online webinars and workshops that will help you quickly get through some of these learning curves. They also have face-to-face mentoring.

There are a number of legal structures that you will choose from when you set up your business, such as sole proprietorship, partnership, and various types of corporations. You will want to consult a qualified legal expert, which I am not, to set up the legal structure that will benefit you most, because each one of these structures will have disadvantages as well as advantages.

An immediate resource that will walk you through these structures, and their advantages and disadvantages, would be SCORE's recorded workshop called "Pros and Cons of the Popular Business Entities: Sole Proprietorship, LLC, S Corp and C Corp." You can go to their website at https://www.score.org/event/pros-cons-popular-business-entities- sole-proprietorship-LLC-SCorp-CCorp. Another excellent resource is Nolo's *The Small Business Start-Up Kit.* You may want to educate yourself as much as possible, and then find a good attorney to help you make your final decision.

Setting up a Fictitious Business Name

Caution: don't ignore local registration requirements. Most cities and many counties require even tiny home-based sole proprietorships to register with them and pay at least a minimum tax.

As a sole proprietor, you can file as yourself using your legal name or invent a name for your company, which is called a fictitious business name. It is called a fictitious business name very simply because it isn't your legal name. If, for example, you're Jay Armstrong doing business as Strong Arm Protection Services, you must file a "fictitious business name" statement with your county showing that your ficticious business name is Strong Arm Protection Services. This is also referred to as a "DBA"—"doing business as."

It may be a public relations point to have a fictitious business name if it presents more of a professional image than just your name would. Depending on your state, your fictitious business name statement may have to be filed with the state's Division of Corporations (as in Florida), with the Recorder/County Clerk (as in California), or possibly with the city government. Services like legalzoom.com will do the work for you for a $99 fee plus the cost of filing. Save the 99 bucks and do this very simple work yourself unless you're too busy making money.

If your business name includes your last name, and the last names of any and all partners, you already have the right to operate under that name without filing any paperwork.

Your bank will let you create a business checking account under a fictitious name. If you want to use your own name, give your bank a call and see if they can give you a business account under that name.

The Legalities of Hiring Subcontractors / Vendors

You can't treat subcontractors as employees unless you want to pay employment tax. In all business transactions, you must treat them as vendors. There is a specific set of rules that you need to adhere to regarding subcontractors. Can you issue orders to them if you're the team lead? Absolutely. Can you issue them an employee manual? You'd better not! Nothing in the paper trail can contradict their vendor status.

The IRS website (https://www.irs.gov/newsroom/understanding-employee-vs-contractor-designation) states: "Classifying an employee as an independent contractor with no reasonable basis for doing so makes employers liable for employment taxes."

There are a number of red flags that can alert the IRS that you should be:

- paying employment taxes and
- withholding federal income tax, Medicare and Social Security from their pay.

As of November 2017, the above-referenced IRS web page, which is in the public domain, spelled out the rules. You can find these rules online on the IRS website. It is very important to take the time to read through these rules, and think them through and understand exactly how they would apply to your business.

The tax laws are complex and not always sensible. Your CPA can help to interpret them for you. It's one of their main functions.

Your Income from Your Business

If your business is structured as a sole proprietorship, you can take a "draw" from your business income for personal expenses. In effect, what you are doing is withdrawing money from your equity—the money you have invested in the way of capital, or are investing in your company in the way of profit. If you are wise, you will only draw when revenue is higher than expenses—when your balance sheet is "in the black." If you draw too much away, you won't be able to pay your bills, or reinvest in your business.

Taxes

With a sole proprietorship, you calculate the net income of the business using a Schedule C for income tax purposes. Then you include that amount on your 1040, which is your personal income tax return. The business will have to pay self-employment taxes (Social Security and Medicare) on the net income, which will be the business income minus the expenses of the business. Your draw is not taxed.

Insurance

You will also have to determine what kind of insurance you will need. It depends on what the client requires. Liability insurance is often required unless you are working under someone else's license and insurance. Minimums would be half a million to a million dollars; however, some clients may insist on more. Your state may require your business to be incorporated. Bigger clients may also have specific legal requirements, so make sure that question is taken up in the discovery process.

Executive Protection Licenses, Permits & Badges

There are certain legal basics that you simply can't afford to neglect. It's especially important to "be legal" in our business of executive protection, where our efforts have to be aligned with those of law enforcement.

Your "starter package" will include whatever licenses are required to operate an executive protection business in your state. In Florida, we learn these requirements by consulting the Department of Agriculture or the Division of Licensing.

Federal licenses & permits? Don't worry about them at the early stages of your business; you'll have your hands full establishing a thriving local and regional practice.

With certain specialties, your license will include a badge. The license is typically issued by the state. The state can license you for concealed carry, open carry, private investigator, chauffeur, and the like.

The licensing classifications and requirements vary so much from state to state and year to year that I won't try to list them. Be sure to know and understand your state's rules, regulations, and laws. Keep in mind which states and countries you will be traveling in, and know their laws. Make sure your network includes individuals familiar with the laws and cultures of any place you might be asked to work. Remember that "connections are king" in this industry.

The state issues your license; you get the badge made to order. It should bear the same distinctive shield or logo that you use on your business card and your LinkedIn profile. You'll wear it on those occasions when you need to present a hard target; usually you'll just carry it and show it on demand. This is part of branding yourself.

Your logo must not bear any resemblance to the state seal. Nonetheless, the public tends to respect—or fear—anyone wearing a badge. This works to our advantage sometimes, but we never misrepresent ourselves. Badges can be counterfeited, or you can flash a PI badge and say you're a cop, but these are really bad and illegal ideas. A criminal investigation for fraud would spell the end of your business.

Some states are so strict that it is nearly impossible to do any type of security or bodyguard work. Some cities have laws that differ from the state's laws, and vice versa. Learn what you need to know about the different jurisdictions. Don't assume.

Do not be an unlicensed operator. This will backfire as soon as somebody asks for your credentials.

8

Market Like a Master

The one thing that I love to do is market like a master. I love marketing and seeing results. If you're not actively marketing, you will not be at the top of your game. Everything has to do with marketing. You are your own brand, so you must walk around like a billboard. What you portray and what people see is exactly what they will believe. Perception is reality.

Before you start to market yourself, do you believe in yourself? All of your best marketing ideas will come to you because you truly believe in your capability and capacity to make a difference. You will find your opportunities to make that difference right there in your chosen "location, location, location."

What is your brand? Who are you? To market a product is to sell the benefits of that given product. Once you are sold on the benefits of said product and you use the product, now you believe and trust that product. In this case you and your competence are the products. So you have to really be honest with yourself and do not over-sell and under-deliver.

Educate the Public

In my prior book, I discussed the "bodyguard myth," the idea that working as a bodyguard is a glamorous job, that you will be Kevin Costner guarding a famous singer, a character right out of a movie script. This myth works against anyone trying to make a living at executive protection.

The public needs to understand our profession, recognize what we do, how it's different from police protection, and why it's sometimes the only answer. We're not bouncers. We may be tough guys (and gals), but we're also *smart* guys and gals. Yes, we can fight, but we're not spoiling for a fight. We want the client to have an uneventful day. For celebrities and other public figures, an uneventful day is priceless!

If you're tough enough to ward off all threats by intimidation alone, while putting everyone else at ease with your calm assurance, that's a battle won without fighting. Most of the time it is the pre-planning and advance work that makes this possible.

If all of us in the EP world work together to help the public to understand the service we provide, and if we do good work and make our clients look good, *we* look good.

High Profile or Low Profile?

You have to stay visible to prospective clients and within the industry. On the other hand, as a CPO, you must maintain a low profile for your clients. Everything is on a "need to know" basis. A celebrity's whereabouts is considered news. Reporters and paparazzi go to considerable lengths to track their locations and routes. If the celebrity doesn't want the information known, you must protect it. You play it cagey. *You certainly don't brag about the detail on social media.* You don't say who you're working for, or even who you've worked for in the past, without their knowledge and permission. This is critical to understand when you are marketing yourself.

You're dealing with different publics. It's a good exercise to make a list of these publics and define your responsibilities to them. Make sure your subcontractors understand these relationships too.

Hustle Marketing

Hustle marketing is what I do. It is "Get off your ass and get out there and do anything that you have to do to get your name out there." The tendency is to say, "Here's my business card, call me." Change that approach to, "Give me your name and number and I'm going to call you."

Hustle marketing, when I owned a martial arts school, was going to events, fairs, festivals, putting flyers on cars, going door to door and putting doorhangers on their doorknobs—but never breaking the law. Hustle marketing is something that you have to push yourself to do. That means to heel-toe it. Walk and talk. That's hustle marketing. Then, once you understand what they want, you can sell them on what they want.

Search Engine Marketing

I'm going to introduce some terms here that you absolutely must understand if you're going to succeed in today's market.

Browser: a computer program that provides the user with various internet-related services, such as searching for websites, accessing them, and navigating them. Browsers also provide services such as email, and uploading and downloading documents, videos and audio files. Examples of popular browsers are Chrome, Firefox and Safari.

Search engine: a browser-based program that searches the World Wide Web for matches to one or more keywords. Examples of this are Google, DuckDuckGo and Bing.

Keywords: terms used in a search.

Search query: a user's request to look up a combination of keywords. Optimization: making something the best it can be (the optimum).

Search engine optimization (SEO): increasing the odds that a search engine will find your website when a particular combination of keywords is searched. This is done by writing or rewriting your website content so it is "relevant" to those keywords.

At this writing, my website—internationalep.com—comes up third out of 19,700,000 web pages in a Google search for "executive protection."

Google typically shows ten results per page, so my site has "first page ranking," which is great because most people don't take the time to look at page after page of results. If they find a good match on the first page, that's usually as far as they will go.

But your startup EP agency doesn't need to be found by the whole world. If you're in Seattle, it doesn't even help to have people in New York looking you up. It's a lot easier and cheaper to achieve visibility using such keywords as "Executive Protection Seattle."

With SEO, the only person you pay is the one who rewrites your website content and keeps tweaking it (over a period of several months) until you get the desired result.

There's also a second stage of search engine marketing, which is paying for ads to appear when people search for your chosen combination of keywords. In the case of Google searches, this service is called Google AdWords. The person you hire to do your SEO can handle your paid search ads as well.

Social Media

Besides search engine marketing, you also need to be visible on Facebook and LinkedIn. The person you hire for search engine marketing won't necessarily be an expert in social media, and vice versa. But if they are, that's an added bonus.

If you're having trouble finding the right person for your Internet marketing, call me and I'll offer my opinion. I'm no more of a website expert than you are, but I have a system that is working.

Branding

What is the one thing that makes you buy a certain product? If you can answer this question you can sell your own brand to others. Let's examine this for a minute. You buy certain brands for certain reasons. Can you name a few?

The reason we buy products is because we believe in them. We trust that product. The product makes us feel proud or happy or secure, or helps our survival in specific ways.

There is power in your words: the power of visualization; the power of persistence. This is branding: you help your potential client visualize you meeting their needs, and you persist with presenting that vision. If you believe in yourself and your competence, you can sell yourself. You are the product, you are the producer that makes others feel secure. If you don't believe in yourself, why should anyone else?

Your Brand Is You

People have to believe in your product. The first thing you present is you; you follow that up with your communicated vision—words and images.

Consider your appearance, hygiene, mannerisms. How you present yourself determines how you will be perceived. Even if you offer the best and most reliable protection in your region, people won't know it unless you look the part.

Judge your audience. Do they prefer a casual, laid-back attitude or a highly professional one? Professional is always safer; you'll know when to relax later on in the relationship.

If you want to work with high-profile clients, you have to be able to adapt to that environment. You should look good, be fit and be clean-cut. Good communication skills are essential. Personality is a huge part of being successful in this business. You must be adaptable and flexible, able to adjust your personality to the client, situation, and threat.

Get over the idea of being a "famous bodyguard," if you ever had it. Where you want name recognition is within the business. You want to be known by colleagues who might hire you or be hired by you.

Just do great work and don't miss a chance to make the fact known to those who need to know.

The wannabe "bodyguard to the stars" will never get a chance to specialize in a *type* of client until they have protected hundreds of clients of all kinds. If you turn away legitimate work because it isn't glamorous enough, good luck staying in business long enough to attract the high-end client.

There aren't enough celebrity details to go around. The only way to get to Hollywood as a bodyguard is to prove exceptional skills. And even then— as I repeat again and again because it is that important— "connections are king."

Managing Your Brand

Developing a personal brand is similar to product branding. The overall goal with branding is to differentiate yourself (the product) in the market so you can attain your objectives. Compare your business to a successful one in the same space. What is that guy delivering? Can I match it? Do I need to carve out a niche at a lower price point or simply deliver a superior product?

The process of branding includes defining your brand and brand attributes, positioning your brand in a different way than your competitors and then managing all aspects of your personal brand. Discover what makes you stand out from the competition and make that part of your message.

Determine Your Brand Attributes

What type of detail are you particularly good at? What unique qualities do you bring to the table? A crucial step of marketing your services is to work out a clear statement—your unique value proposition (UVP). (Some marketers call it the "unique selling proposition.") *Unique* means different from everyone else. What differentiates you from the competition? If you can be reached 24/7, if you can grab your go-bag and be on the detail in two hours flat, there's a competitive advantage. A fairly high percentage of the opportunities that come my way have to be delivered *now now now*, and that is one of my brand attributes.

How will you advertise your business? Depends on demographics and your chosen niche. My business model looks like an Easter egg basket: a bunch of little eggs and a few big eggs. The ones who keep coming back are what keep you in business.

Research and Strategizing

The biggest issue I see when it comes to personal branding is a lack of adequate research and strategizing. There's a good reason that "Ready, aim, fire" is done in that sequence. You'd be amazed how many new businesses brand themselves in a "Fire, ready, aim" sequence.

Why? I submit that it's because they think they are already known and that they have something to build on, when in all likelihood they are unknown in the community of prospective clients that they plan to serve—whether well-known in their personal circles or not.

People tend to get so excited that they forget to do their homework before taking action.

You need to determine who is buying this type of service, and what do they want? Market research is the process of gathering and analyzing data to determine which products and services are in demand. The next step is to strategize how to adjust your offering to respond to what is needed, and how to communicate your capabilities that meet those needs.

Market research can provide valuable insight to help you:

- Reduce business risks
- Spot current and upcoming problems in the industry
- Identify sales opportunities

One of the best ways I learn is by watching and studying other people or their companies fail. I try to make sure I don't do anything that I just watched or witnessed or learned that these other companies are doing. This is a great way that fighters learn. You get knocked out, you're learning something. Learning from other people's mistakes saves me a lot of time.

We spend all this time, knowledge and supplies protecting other people. As CEOs rather than CPOs, we now have to protect ourselves and our own assets. If not, we're a failing industry. The industry will be looked at in a much brighter way if there are more successful professionals in the industry. If there are too many weekend warriors who dummy-down the process, the pricing, the negotiations, or the image, they will make the industry itself look bad.

Part of this is knowing who is already working in your area at the same business. If you realize that there are far more people who need protection than resources to serve them, you won't worry about competition. Network with your colleagues and peers. Find opportunities to work with them, find like-minded CPOs who are good team players, and you've got a head start toward being successful in your area.

Get a Testimonial

Whenever clients are happy with your team's performance, collect a testimonial. Study your last few testimonials. What benefit of working with you keeps being mentioned? Say that on your Facebook and Linked-In profiles.

You have to find at least one thing that sets you apart and remind people of it in all your marketing messages. This helps build your value in the public mind. As you collect testimonials, keep a tally of the points your clients keep mentioning, and your best attributes will emerge.

When somebody is blown away by the speed and quality of your service, get a testimonial right then. Occasionally someone will write a really nice testimonial letter you can use in your marketing. Others may be just as thrilled, but the moment gets away and other demands take its place. In that case, write what you think they might say, and see if you can persuade them to either tweak it or approve it "as-is."

You have to believe in yourself. Confidence is the key to your success.

Make sure you're good at everything you do—and when you get praise, accept it! Where others see perfection, you may be stuck on the little goofs that could have gotten you in trouble (but didn't). Be the other person for a second. Like what you see (through their eyes). Convert their praise into a written success story if at all appropriate.

Determining What to Charge

As part of marketing, you will need to determine what you are going to charge for your services.

To get your prices right when you are just starting out, you can call security companies around you or in the area you will be operating in. You might say, "I need a bodyguard. My wife's going to fly out there," and get their prices, and now you have a base price. There's another way, and that is to find out what off-duty police charge. Base it off of them.

If you are doing the detail, you're getting all the money. If you give it to a sub-contractor, then you have to pay him and keep a enough for yourself to run the office. There are a lot of moving parts: rent, insurance, office, vehicles. As long as you have someone you can work with and talk to and negotiate a deal with, it will always work.

Variables in Pricing

Prices will depend very much on circumstances, and each job will be bid accordingly. Someone calls us up and tells us they need security. We have certain criteria that we follow. We know how much we need to make it work. There is never a specific percentage that I keep. I know what I need, per man hour of a detail, to keep the office running. That is something you will have to determine—how much per billable hour you will need to keep.

There's a few things that I take into consideration when determining the price of a detail:

- Is the threat high or low?
- Is the risk high or low?
- Armed or unarmed?
- Are we going to be covert or are we in uniform?
- Do we need a vehicle?
- Static or dynamic? (moving about and being an executive protection agent)
- Do they need a team of people?

- Do you need me RIGHT NOW? If it is "right now," the price goes up. If it is, "Hey, I need you in a couple of weeks," price stays the same.
- Short-term contract, the price goes up.
- Long-term contract, the price goes down.
- What city are we in? In California, and large cities like New York or Miami, we get paid much more. That is what they are used to, so you have to elevate the prices to pay the guards what they are used to being paid. But in Georgia, Nebraska, we don't get paid much.

It is also possible to have a high threat and a low risk at the same time. The threat is very, very high, but it might be in New York and we are in Miami, so the risk is low. If we are neighboring counties, that is high threat, high risk. So we take that into consideration as well.

What you are looking at is billable hours, that will give you the total amount for your team, and how much net you are going to make. We have "A guards," "B guards" and "C Guards. "A guards" are my best guards. They get paid much more. Say we're just watching a parking lot. I'll put a "C guard" there.

So you take all that into consideration. How much travel time you have, how much do you need per diem. If it is a static post, houses, car dealerships, apartment buildings, those are low risk and the prices are generally the same.

We just want to be competitive because we are going up against people who underbid us all the time. When people want to underbid us, my question is to the client or the customer, if you pay them peanuts, you're going to get monkeys. We pay our guards more because we expect more from them. We never decrease our prices. We always increase our value. That is something I learned a long time ago. When people want to negotiate something with me, they might say, "Can you come down a little bit?" My response is, do you want me to put a less-qualified guard there? I let them answer their own questions.

Can I help them out? Yes, I can always have wiggle room to make the deal go through. But I always try to increase what we have. For X amount of money, you are getting an off-duty or retired officer, he's been trained in X, Y and Z.

We pay the guard a range, depending on who the guard is, what the location is, is armed or not, is it static or dynamic or doing something that is more high-level. Sometimes we can go above what a police officer gets because with us, we are also involved in customer service as well as protection.

Contact your prospects, get quotes out, get business in, get better and better at delivering. Charge more than the competition if you can, but make sure you really are that much better—and then some. Work on every point that you can control. Speed of service and promptness of response are **huge** toward being the first vendor they choose. Don't keep a potential customer waiting for a quote. Take that call on Sunday. Make sure your business phone forwards to your cell phone.

9

How to Succeed in Sales

Sales can be very challenging. You have to understand its distinct parts:

- prospecting (developing leads wherever you can find them)
- qualifying the prospect (finding out if they're a good fit, and can pay)
- discovery (learning their exact needs and their buying process/power)
- closing the sale (removing all obstacles to a "yes" and getting the signature).

This chapter will take you through the sales process and give you time-honored, successful techniques. The next chapter will focus more in depth specifically on how to negotiate the contract.

Each sales call you make will be different and can be filled with challenges. I'm going to recommend that you set up a process to learn from each challenging call. Write down the obstacle you ran into, and what the outcome was.

Did you close the deal? If not, how could you have closed the deal? Did you use the bubble theory—asking questions until you truly understood that person's unique considerations? Did you record your conversation, and go back and listen to your own voice? How did you sound? Were you smiling while talking? Simply putting a smile on your face can make your conversational tone friendlier and more engaging.

Seasoned negotiators and communicators understand that sales is simply a numbers game, and more importantly, know how to use "numbers" to propel themselves towards their objective. For them, sales is more of a process than it is a task. And in all honesty, *you* must love what you do, love what you are selling and believe in yourself. You, your services, your talents and advice are the product.

It's important to understand the basic steps common to most sales cycles, and that is what we will cover here.

How to Reach Your Income Target

What does it mean that sales is simply a numbers game?

Understanding Billable Hours

First you need to determine what your income goal is and how to get there. Once you've accumulated some history, you will better understand what your net earnings will be on a typical job, and use that to determine how how many jobs you need to do in a year to meet your income target. As covered in the prior section called Variables in Pricing, you will have determined the amount from each billable hour that you need to keep your office running. So you are really calculating the number of billable hours you need to meet your income target. When you are just starting out, you may not yet know these numbers. This is where a mentor would be extremely helpful—someone with experience in the executive protection businesses.

Realistic Time Management

One thing you are going is coming up with an estimation of how much of everything needs to be done and in what time period in order to meet your targets. You will figure out how many proposals you need to make to result in a closed sale. For example, you may need to make five proposals to result in one detail. If you determine that you need to accomplish at least 10 details in a year to meet your net income goal, that is 50 proposals in a year, which is about one a week, based on 250 work days a year.

Now you need to determine how many face-to-face appointments you need to make before you have a prospect to make a proposal to. If that is two appointments, then you will be making 100 appointments a year.

That is 2.5 appointments a week, so you would aim for 3 appointments a week.

Next you need to find out how many prospecting calls you will need to complete in order to get those appointments. If you need to make ten calls to get one appointment, that is 25 calls per week. This is about five calls per working day. But it may take a lot more than that.

So this gives you a sense of how to allot your time as a CEO. This allows you to design your day with much more focus. Seeing a number like "five calls a day" or "three appointments per week" or "one proposal a week," you get a good sense of how to manage your time.

Prospecting

The sales process begins by *looking for the client*. It involves identifying potential customers. It involves determining whether they are actually qualified to be a client.

The first thing to understand is what kind of client is a good fit for your business. How will you know a client is a good match for your services?

1. Your skill set meets their needs.
2. They can carry on a reasonable conversation.
3. They don't haggle about price.
4. There is a chance of multiple assignments.

Do I demand all four of these qualities? No, of course not.

One of the keys to a good business model is knowing how you're going to handle exceptions.

1. If the client needs something you don't normally provide, you can subcontract that aspect of the job. Maybe a female CPO is speci- fied. Have some in your network.
2. If the client is a battered woman, she may be hysterical or medi- cated or both. In a case like that, you have to take responsibility for both ends of the conversation. Put yourself in her shoes, be patient and draw the information out of her.
3. Deals that automatically go to the lowest bidder generally aren't worth it to me. But in a case of genuine need, where the

individual is deserving, I may do a detail *pro bono*. I had a witness protection case like that. Pro bono work is a good networking and reputation- building activity.

4. Some types of details are repeating, such as the celebrity escort. Great! Get as many of these as you can. But I would never turn a detail down just because it's a one-off.

Leads & Opportunities

When you're looking for business, go where the threats are. Seek out the people and activities that are at risk: politicians, jewelry stores, clients of domestic violence clinics. These people are going to need help. Seek out divorce attorneys and spousal abuse attorneys. If you have an attorney, ask him for leads, ask him for referrals to colleagues. Go to some of those places, get in front of those people, and talk about your brand, your unique value proposition.

Referrals and Testimonials

Referrals are a huge thing. I ask for referrals. I ask for testimonials. Part of being successful is people believing in you and trusting you. If they believe in you and trust you, they'll pass your information along. Over-deliver, earn people's trust, build up their confidence. Network with them, find common interests to talk about, become their friend. People want to help people they trust. By keeping all your commitments, you are continuously building trust.

I get a lot of well-paying contracts because I have earned the trust of my colleagues in the industry and I never go back on my word. One of the biggest deals I ever made was on a handshake, and to this date the mutual trust remains.

Your character will be your major selling point. Who are your character references? Previous clients. They may not want their identities known, but you can sometimes get an anonymous testimonial, or one from a client's handler.

The Warm-Up: Direct Mail Marketing

I use direct-mail marketing to take the freeze out of a cold call. I have done this for 20-plus years. You are actually sending information to specific potential clients. By taking this approach you increase your odds of the potential client already having some awareness of your services when you call, which may lead to a more favorable conversation.

Sales Calls Preparation

1. Define your purpose. What do you want to achieve?
2. Prepare questions. What do you need to ask?
3. Prepare answers. Summarize answers to likely questions.
4. Practice. Use a voice recorder to hear how you come across.
5. Visualize. Put up a picture of your caller or another person. Imagine you are talking to a person rather than a disembodied voice.
6. Zone in. Get a picture of their "problems" threat in your mind. Envi- sion you are talking to them as a person and not a client. Use your human nature to be at their temperature and to not overexcite them or under-care, but to truly zone in on their fears.

Put yourself in a position to interview your potential clients, by phone or face to face. You will need to ask them the questions necessary to understand their needs and identify their threats.

The Fortune Is in the Follow Up!

You have to follow through! Get all the contact information up front: name, phone number, email address, street address. On any calls or inquiries, do not stop asking for the sale until the answer is "No" or they have someone else. Their kid could have been sick, their cat died, they could have been distracted. It could just be timing.

There is a financial advisor who has been calling me for seven years. Each time, I tell him to call me back in six months. I sat down with him once, but I really didn't like what he had to offer. I said, "No, at this time I don't need your services, but check back with me in six months." If his offering changes to better fit my needs, I would do business with him, because he has always followed up.

Be "Johnny on the spot." That means to be available, fully, when you are needed. This is a customer service business, period. One good deal can be all you need to sink your teeth into and really push forward. Or have 10 small deals or 100 smaller ones. Just close the deals!

Whether we want to admit it or not, we are always selling ourselves in one way or another. Fortunately, people want to be sold. They need your services. The only way to be hired or find the dream account is to be proactive and show you can serve the client. Don't rely on luck. Luck is nothing more than "opportunity meeting preparedness." Are you prepared?

Will you get the deal? Will your efforts pay off? The highest paid sales people in America get paid between $150,000 and $300,000 per year or more. Some of the most successful people in the sales industry simply make one more phone call than all the others.

A number of studies have been done about how many times you have to call a prospect before you make a deal. The usual conclusion is that it takes seven touches to get a deal. In real estate I've heard as high as seventeen touches. But the vast majority of salesmen give up on a prospect within three or four attempts.

Remember, you are your own product. This will hold true even if you have a huge agency with hundreds of employees and a book of standard operating procedures. They're standard because they're the same actions that got you to that level.

Clients don't automatically understand the requirements of a proposed detail. They need to be educated to the benefits of your services, or as I have explained, "pre-frame" them and manage their expectations. They have a threat, a problem, or a need to prevent any problems, and they want to trust you with solving it. Or they're smart and want to be proactive. If they're dealing with an immediate threat, they want reassurance, comfort. They don't know the mechanics of how you'll deliver that. Educate them on the most basic facts. If they're still clinging to the bodyguard myth, paint a more accurate picture for them. Don't assume they know what you know.

Remember, you are the brand. You and your team, whatever team you can assemble fast enough to get the contract, must represent your standards to the world. Your personnel need to know what the brand message is and make it their own. Your leadership is what inspires them to deliver at that level.

Qualifying the Prospect

There are some things you need to ask up front. This is the step where you are determining if this is a legitimate client that you want to take on.

1. Are you speaking with the decision maker?
2. Is there a partner?
3. Is this a family affair?
    a. Is there a wife or husband to deal with?
    b. Are grown children involved in the decision making?
4. Do they have a certain budget?
5. Is this for a company or personal?
6. Is this short term or long term?

Armed with the answers to these questions, you can screen out deals that wouldn't be a good fit for both you and the client. Some deals will never close because of complications on the client's end. Watch for red flags that indicate they're hiding something. Some prospects will never pay you enough to cover your costs, let alone make a profit.

The next process is *discovery*, a whole different set of questions to determine the scope of work which will be specified in your *proposal*.

Interview the Potential Client

The initial prospecting call is not where discovery takes place. Your goal in prospecting is to set an appointment, not to close a sale—though that may happen on occasion, when the needs are very simple.

You've done some qualifying in the prospecting call, screening out the looky-loos and the prospects you can't help or don't want to. The next step is to secure an appointment. I tend to use urgency and be Johnny-on-the-spot. Showing urgency on my end lets them know that they are a priority. The response from the potential client will give you a hint as to whether this is going to be a "hard yes" or a "hard no," a "soft yes" or a "soft no" (which can be developed into a "yes").

When you set up a time or appointment with clients, give people options. Therefore you broaden what you provide for them. You aren't giving them one thing. You are not saying, I'm going to have one guard with one outfit and one look, and one everything. We have multiple things that we can do. And once I give them options of what I can provide, I give them options for setting up meetings as well: Which is better for you, 3:00 on Tuesday or 6:00 on Thursday?

Agreeing to an appointment is generally a sign of interest on the part of your prospect and one step closer to closing the deal. You must not hang onto the disappointments. Learn from them for the next phone call, the next face-to-face meeting or the next email.

When you take a meeting, don't be afraid of failure. Don't run away from it. Run towards it. Your first step will take you to the next step, and every step will bring you closer to goal. Be aggressive toward your goals, but not overbearing when negotiating agreements or contracts.

Don't be afraid of trying to make the deal. There's only one way to find out if you are going to get the next contract, and that is to get the scope of work specified through the discovery process.

Discovery

Once you've qualified the prospect, a new round of questioning begins. What do they need and want? What is the problem they are trying to solve? What is the scope of work?

You'll want to develop your own set of discovery questions based on your circumstances, but this should help you get started:

- Who are the protectee(s)?
- High or low threat?
- High or low risk?
- High or low profile client?
- Short or long term coverage?
- Armed or unarmed guards?
- Covert or overt security?
- Hard or soft target?
- How many CPO's needed?
- Static security, escort or both?
- What hours?
- What locations?
- What routes?
- Expected hazards or conditions?

Some questions can be answered by the prospect, such as what hours is the protection needed. For other questions, such as how many CPO's will be needed, your own experience will be the determining factor.

Get all this mapped out and work out a timeline. Express all that in your proposal. Do it well enough and you might not have to go back and forth several times with revisions.

Managing Expectations

Managing client expectations is vital in sales and in every other aspect of dealing with the public. Know what you can deliver, and communicate that accurately, so that what happens matches what is expected to happen. From the initial interview, you have to educate the client in what is and isn't included in your protection services. Once I establish that framework with a client, I promise a level of service that is more than acceptable to the client. Then I over-deliver. It's quite a reputation builder to go above and beyond the acceptable standard.

This sets an example for subordinates on a detail. The leader always brings his "A" game, or he soon won't have any clients. I drive myself and then the team. I don't let them slack off when there's no immediate action. Everyone's responsible to keep observing and to communicate any change that is observed.

If I were to say to a client, customer, or team, I am going to build this house in three days, then their expectations are, within three days. So I have to manage, direct or mold their expectations: I have to give them a realistic outcome of what is going to happen. I don't want them to think we're going to show up with machine guns, grenades, things of that nature. We're going to come in as professionals, but we can only do so much. So I don't want them to think that we can go further than what we can actually do. I manage their expectations so that they are not let down.

I am managing expectations in four areas: client, customer, team, and students. Let's define these categories. A client is a person. A customer would be more like a business, an establishment, an estate. The customer might be the handler or the company that hired me. The customer might be a big company where they say, we need you to patrol this area, or do EP for the CEOs walking back and forth with money. The team, of course, is the detail that I have hired. And the students are those whom I teach at IEP.

If you manage their expectations, you always keep them at a high point, a happy point. The client may expect me to smack everybody around, or push people out of the way. I can't do that. So I have to explain to him, "This is how we are going to go about it" so he understands. And that is managing his expectations, so he doesn't say, "Go do this" and "Go do that."

I also manage the expectations of my students so they don't think they are going to walk out of the training camp and think that they are bulletproof. For example, I say, "Listen, I don't want to set you up with a false sense of security. When we do tactical gun takeaway and defense, realistically, if you are six feet away from me, I can't do anything. I say, "Within three feet, you can do something. Outside of that, it is very dangerous."

The Proposal

A key part of the sales process is writing and presenting a proposal spelling out your proposed scope of services and the price, with some provision for changes that may come up, such as additional days, additional equipment or additional personnel.

The proposal is what you are selling. It specifies what you will promise to do in the agreement. You'll include an estimated price, and a statement that changes or add-ons will be subject to additional fees.

Get the scope of work agreed on before you settle into price negotiations.

Make sure the prospect has studied the proposal in detail, marking it up with any questions or concerns, before you sit down for the interview. If you arrive at the prospect's office with a proposal they haven't read, prepare to waste half an hour watching them read it.

Negotiating a Price

I heard awhile back, "We don't get paid for what we do, we get paid for what we might have to do." I found this quote to be amazing, and this is why I remembered it and keep it close to me.

A lot of people try to talk us down in price. I'm an armed guard. I have a bullet-proof vest on. I'm going to get paid a certain amount of money. $1000 a day. The client goes, "$1000 a day?" My response is that it's not what I appear to be doing that you are paying me for, which by outward appearances seems to be nothing. It's what I might have to do.

It is just like a doctor on standby. He's not doing anything, but he's still getting paid. But as soon as someone arrives whose life is on the line, he is the critical factor to that person's existence. He has put in years of training and sacrifice to be able to be the difference between life or death for a patient at any given moment. It is the same with executive protection work. You are paying me for what I am trained, willing and fully able to do, and that is to protect and save lives. I may look relaxed, but I am always alert, always ready and able to deliver.

Let's say I'm watching a billionaire's estate. Most of the time it's surrounding by walls, cameras, we're doing perimeter checks, it's very calm. So they ask, "Why are we paying you this much?" My answer is, "It may look outwardly like we're not doing much. You're paying me for what I might have to do," which is put my life on the line, cover and evacuate the client, protect the family, make sure the threat is stopped, or even put my body in the line of a bullet. You are paying for my business accumen to assemble and manage a quality, trained team that is where they need to be, when they need to be there, doing what they need to be doing.

In this industry we either move at a breakneck speed, or nothing's happening. Our value is in our expertise: our ability to handle danger, and our ability to keep our clients away from danger. Part of our value is seeing that nothing happens and being ready if it does. So keep this in mind when negotiating a price.

Whenever possible, don't be the one to name a price. Let them say it first. When the prospect asks me a question, I tend to answer with a question. I'm learning what they want so I can sell them what they want. Every detail is a custom quote. Know the market value, and tailor it to each job.

If you ask the right questions, you can figure out how much they are willing to spend without asking point-blank. You can shoot yourself in the foot by throwing out a dollar amount before you fully understand the situation. You might be ridiculously low and come off as an amateur. At the other extreme, the prospect might expect top-level work at security guard wages.

If you haven't blown them off with a high price, you can work on adjusting their expectations. You may even discover that they only need two guards when they thought they needed five. If the budget they have to spend is a bit more than you really need, you can build more value into the proposal, or over-deliver, rather than bid lower.

If you already know their budget, you can say, "It's well within the figure we discussed," or, "For the amount you've budgeted, I have (number of guards) watching the perimeter/clients for (number of days)."

Know your market; negotiate your target price for scope of services and what I call your "drop dead" terms, as I will explain here. I always know where I need to be cost-wise to put a great team together. I also have to clarify the need for my value. If the client does not listen to my recommendations and see the threat through my eyes, we have a problem. I won't jeopardize my team or my reputation. I also have to balance manpower against profit. Once I take that all into consideration, I have a drop-dead price—the price that ensures I can do the job to my standards.

Some EP agencies will bid low to get the business and then sell the contract to another agency, but then quality control goes out the window and their reputation follows.

I see that as a losing proposition. At that low a price, I would rather move on to a bigger, more profitable deal. There are always more prospects, so don't fixate on one just because the conversation has already been started.

It's imperative to profile and outline all aspects of the contract. Get as much information as you can ahead of time. Before I go to any meeting, I will have already worked out my agenda and will have my notes with me to refer to.

If I cannot express my value to their satisfaction—if, for example, it has to be approved by the board and attorneys and then renegotiated at a later date—I suspect one of two things:

- they aren't serious, or
- they won't end up paying what I need.

I never burn that bridge: I stay in contact, continue to be interested in their situation and their needs.

If they decide they can't afford me, they may settle for a lower bid from one of my competitors. In that case, I may end up getting their business at a later date, if they're not happy with the results.

Once the prospect has agreed that your price is acceptable, it's time to close the deal. Don't assume you have already closed it when you hear "It all looks good." What that really means is "It all looks good, but…"

How to Close the Deal

If you did a thorough job of qualifying the customer and have now designed a proposal that matches the customer's needs and handling any objections, then you should be all set to close the deal. Be confident and ask for the business.

If you missed any of the earlier steps, you'll have to backtrack and get it done properly. Otherwise you'll waste time trying to close a deal that they can't pay for, isn't what they wanted, or is beyond your scope to deliver.

Here are some time-honored closing techniques that work well if the qualifying and discovery steps have been done properly.

The Assumptive Close

"When would you like to start?" or "When would you like this to begin?"

The assumptive close skips "yes or no." You assume the answer is yes and move on to the specifics of getting started.

This works when they've already made up their minds, and it's a relief to the client to move on from decision to action. If there are still any objections, this gets them into the open, so it's a win for you either way.

Handling Objections

You need to be fully prepared to handle any objections that are in the client's mind. Dealing with objections is actually a way of getting the deal sealed. You have to be able to think on your feet, and of course you have to be dealing with someone who can make the decision or at least influence the decision. (If the client is a celebrity, you'll usually be dealing with a handler, who may not have the authority to sign off. You then have to close the handler well enough that he or she will persuade the client to sign off on the deal.)

Think through what objections might be there before entering the meeting or phone conversation with the potential client. Work out in your mind the answers to common objections.

If objections arise that you simply can't work through, then you may not have qualified the prospect well enough. They're not a fit for you, or you're not a fit for them. Don't waste your efforts trying to close an unqualified prospect.

When objections are voiced, you can deal with them. If the prospect really wants the service, then you're both on the same team, working toward a common goal. In the spirit of teamwork, ask the prospect how they would deal with the obstacle under discussion. You should be close to the solution if you used the bubble theory.

You're trying to move the deal forward. If your efforts are met with hesitation, and no objection has been voiced, ask something like this: "Do you have any reason, if we gave you the agreement at this price, that you wouldn't do business with my agency?"

This is Sales 101, yet it took me 20 years to learn.

If the client answers "no" to this question, you have indirectly gotten them to agree to the terms of the agreement. This is preframing, or getting your customer in the frame of mind to be persuaded. If the answer is "yes," you have the opportunity to address objections, revisit their "bubble in their minds," and close the deal.

Test the Close

If you suspect there are objections that haven't been voiced, you can just ask for the business and see what happens. You'll either get the business or you'll get the reasons why not, which you can deal with one by one.

"If I can help you find a way to deal with that issue, can we start on the fifteenth, or would the twentieth be better?"

If they answer that the twenty-first is better, great! You've gotten an answer. Always try to give them a choice instead of a "yes or no" question. But maybe they'll say "I'll let you know after I've talked it over with my (partner, spouse, attorney)." Great! You're moving the process forward. "Okay, Mr. Jones. Now we did establish that you have the authority to sign, correct?"

"Yes, but as a courtesy, I never sign an agreement without (his/her/ their) buy-in."

"I understand. When will you be having that conversation? Okay, let me help you prepare for that. Let's have a ten-minute call the day before." Or failing that, "So the meeting will be Tuesday at 2 p.m. Would you like to conference me in?" If no, "I'll check in with you Tuesday at 3:30, all right? I'll send you a calendar invite."

Work through any objection until you have the solutions that will allow an agreement to move forward. Objections can lead directly into the close if handled skillfully. Anticipate them and turn them to advantage.

Give Options

"Talking with you and understanding all of your requests, I believe these types of services would work. Would you like to go with one CPO or a team? And would you prefer a covert or a hard target?"

This is an effective method of moving the sale forward: give them more options. Get them to say yes to one thing and they can't say no to everything. Obviously they needed you or they wouldn't have called, emailed, or contacted you.

Reinforce Urgency

In executive protection, the urgency of the situation is on your side. You're not selling an expensive phone to someone who has a perfectly good phone. You're solving a problem that isn't going to go away by itself.

Once your proposal is in front of the customer, you should be able to close out the competition by giving them compelling reasons to buy now.

Believe in your product and reinforce the urgency you established in the discovery phase. "Sir or ma'am, I'd hate to see anyone get hurt or feel uncomfortable because we didn't get this protection in place. Would you like to take the next step toward protecting your family today?" Or, "We would like to recommend this protocol to safeguard you."

Fear itself or fear of the unknown is a powerful motivator, but education is more empowering. Remember, you are the expert. What do experts do? Explain their thoughts! This closing tactic is most effective in situations where the consequences of not hiring a CPO will actually harm the business, its CEO, the actor, or the abused woman, simply by allowing the status quo to continue.

Reinforce the urgency with external factors beyond the potential client's control, such as new legislation or economic conditions which may affect them, their family or organization. I have clients all around the world, so I have to pay attention and understand what is happening wherever we operate. Economic conditions in Brazil, for instance, are much different than here in the USA. If economic conditions deteriorate in a country, the economy itself could implode, creating more threats and deaths.

You have to understand where you are going to be: not just the weather, not just the climate, but what is the climate of the people. You have to take the temperature of your threat. The temperature of your threat is all kinds of conditions that exist in a particular area that you have to recognize and deal with. It can be as small a thing (to you) as them seeing your cell phone, and then assuming you are a millionaire. In some countries, they will kill you for your phone. If you are wearing a fancy watch, you're done. So you have to understand the economic climate of where you are going to be because if you go in there dressed in expensive clothes, it's not going to happen. You have to look the part, be the part, become the part. Likewise, the urgency created by the climate where the protection is needed must be explained to the potential client.

You don't want to send a millionaire CEO to Honduras without a CPO, because that would be foolish. You want to have the proper team in place. You want to make sure that wherever your client goes, the advance is already there. So that is how you protect the CEO, the actor, the abused woman instead of simply allowing the status quo to continue.

Most salesmen have to invent gimmicks to create a sense of urgency. This takes a lot of creativity when the product is a newer phone to replace a perfectly good one. In the executive protection world, we don't have that problem. A gentle reminder of the urgency of the situation is usually enough to move the prospect to a decision. Remind them as well that the sooner they implement the security solution, the sooner they will have peace of mind.

Sweeten the Pot

Maybe you have compelling reasons to want the business this week, but for the client, next week is just as good. Offer an incentive that they can't reasonably refuse.

"If I offer a supervisor for free, can we make this work?"

Obviously, not every situation is the same or every closing phrase appropriate. But for important or very large deals, offering an exclusive or time-sensitive add-on to sweeten the pot might be a smart move.

Discounts are a last resort in this type of negotiation. You have good reasons for charging the amount you need. You can build a little bit of negotiating room into the price, but don't give away your profit margin in the stampede to get more business now-now-now. I don't try to underbid my competition. Instead, I position my service as the best, and then I over-deliver.

Verbally Say or Use the Phrase "I Can Guarantee…"

It seems too good to be true. But the truth is, I do guarantee to give my best and do my best. Obviously I cannot guarantee a threat won't happen, but I can guarantee I will do my best to deter it. But never sell a false sense of security. Anything that you can guarantee, keep saying it.

I will continue to emphasize that you must communicate a sense of urgency. Say, "If we finalize this agreement today, I can guarantee we can start immediately. How does that sound? A special advance [information gathering] can be done and handed to you first thing in the morning for your review."

Listen for the solutions, name them, commit to them, and guarantee results. Work backward from the final product, the detail itself. Consider all factors: implementing staff (or the right CPO), additional training involved (if any), non-disclosures, background checks, credit reports. These are all pearls in the final follow up. You can guarantee these factors. And by working backward you bring all these guarantees into the agreement. Include that "The agreement has to be signed by (date) for us to meet your standards." They have to have a start date; if they don't offer one, set it yourself.

Cross the Finish Line

Some deals have to be handed from one person to another or from one attorney to a board, etc. Unfortunately, it can get to be ridiculous. However, with most of my clients, I have pre-framed them, I have gotten inside their "bubble," and I'm in front of the actual decision maker.

Once I have controlled the situation, my next approach is to ask the question that will get a commitment: "When would you like to meet?" "When would you like this to begin?" "How would you like to pay: credit card, PayPal, check?" When you have a positive answer, tell the client, "I can have my office manager email the agreement over and we can sign off right now." If that's not possible, get a firm appointment for the next meeting, when the signing will take place.

You're not creating the need. The need is already there. You're creating a trustworthy image at that prospect's reality level. If your service is awesome, word will spread.

You are increasing trust and reducing any barriers they might have—the contract is already prepared, and it covers all the points you've verbally established with them, so all they need to do is sign.

Clients like the idea of progress. If you establish realistic timeframes, meet your deadlines, and are attentive with customer service, you'll get the repeat business. Pre-frame them about what the experience will be like and they'll feel more comfortable about signing.

From the first prospecting call to the closing meeting, stop any and all procrastination. If it can be done tomorrow, do it today, and if it can be done today, do it NOW! Procrastination is the death of success. Hustle, market, follow up, and follow through. Do it now, not tomorrow; sooner, not later.

Success waits for no one. Success is in your hands and in your determination. Focus on what is in your control and if it is not in your control, try to put it in your control. Remember, only you can control your destiny.

Keep Selling

At what time do you stop selling? Never!

When you're doing all the work yourself, it's tempting to ease back on sales as soon as your calendar is booked with details for a few weeks ahead. That's putting a ceiling on your business, and you'll regret it soon enough.

When a company has at least one full-time salesperson, do they fire him as soon as things start going well? Obviously, you would never do that. So always keep selling as part of your routine. Or if you're so personally involved in a detail that you have to drop everything else, make sure it's temporary. Delegate what you can now, and build your team so you're not indispensable on the front lines.

The Comfort Zone Is the Danger Zone

Don't stop pushing when you get enough work to keep you for a while. Likewise, don't be the go-to guy for every assignment.

Visualize your day in terms of how much outreach you'll accomplish. If you dread picking up the phone, as many salespersons do, discipline yourself to pick it up and dial. Command the hands to reach for the phone, pick it up, put it to the ear, and dial. Repeat. After all, it is you who is in charge. Challenge yourself to an hour a day for the first week. For the second week, an hour and a half a day. Don't grab something that's already easy for you to do and use it as an excuse to put off things that are less interesting or fun.

In fact, I urge you to pick the activity you dread most and tackle it first.

Your Investment in Client Development and Retention

I want you to examine now the hard work and expense it takes to acquire each client. This should help you to understand the value of retaining your clients once you have acquired them.

Keep track of all of the expenses required to get to the table to sign each client until you truly understand this initial outflow of time and money that goes toward client development. Track the cost, at your hourly rate—the time for phone calls and emails, the time to prepare your presentation, travel time. Add expenses: meals, entertainment, copies, postage, etc.

The benefit of tracking this information is twofold. First, when your next opportunity arises, and you refer to this itemization, you will have a good idea of what personal outflow will be necessary to get that next client. Second, seeing your value on paper, in black and white, should serve as a great motivation to build your client base and then retain them.

So, as you can see from this exercise, once you get your client, the goal is to keep them. Invest your time, energy and attention in that client. Once you have sold your product and now have prospects for repeat business, overinvest in them.

Keep in mind that a client is a person. Treat them as such. Clients have families, children, mothers, fathers, etc. Be very conscious to maintain your position as CEO by providing exemplary customer service in your commitment to your client. I don't care how you slice the pie; customer service is the fundamental key to success in this industry. It costs zero to have manners, to be polite, and to be responsive. Be humble and gracious. If you don't provide positive, respectful energy (service), someone else will.

10

Contract Negotiation

Negotiating a contract is a precise skill in itself so I have given it a separate chapter. First, I will give an overview, and then get into specifics.

I like the word "agreement" much better than "contract" when speaking to a client, because "contract" has a harder sound. For exactly that reason, I'm going to call it "agreement" in this section.

In business, especially this industry, it is imperative to negotiate your contract to keep you safe and away from the court systems—and to avoid paying huge attorney fees to keep you out of court. The information in this chapter is in no way a substitute for retaining an attorney who can sniff out shady deals. Ultimately, before you sign any major deals, the contract should be reviewed by your attorney.

Keep in mind that attorneys are deal breakers, not deal makers. It is their job to spot the flaws in a contract that could lead to difficulties. The more they can find wrong with a deal, the longer they stay employed. My attorney reads it, takes something out. Their attorney reads it, adds something, which changes the paragraph. This can go on far too long. The person who wants the deal done, has to talk to the attorney and say, listen, there has to be a line that we stop at. And everybody has to meet in the middle. Because both attorneys don't want to cave in. But I want the deal done. At some point I have to negotiate it myself, and let the attorneys say, this is the best we can do. It's up to you to push for a resolution both sides can accept.

If you have to pay an attorney, do it to avoid trouble up front, not to get you out of trouble that could have been avoided.

A true contract is binding with signatures, witnesses, and a notary. It is "black and white," unambiguous. With a security or executive protection contract, it acts like a living, breathing document. It should take into account that circumstances are constantly changing: destinations, scope of services, multiple clients. Make sure there are provisions for such changes.

Examine the contract and flag anything that is ambiguous (that could be interpreted more than one way) and find a clearer way to say it. In most cases the first draft will come from the CPO.

Find out if your potential client has a standard EP agreement they want you to sign. That's more likely to come up with celebrities or really large organizations. If this comes up, have your attorney review it and make sure you don't underbid.

Start with a good template that has your attorney's blessing and covers anything that can be reasonably expected to come up. Delete paragraphs that don't apply. Run it by the client, and get very alert if they return something that is extensively red-lined. Is that just because their attorney wants to earn his fee? Are they trying to put you in a position where they can weasel out later on some technicality? Anything you don't understand, you flag it and take it up with your own attorney.

Even the most airtight contract is no substitute for good faith and trust on both sides. I'm not going to advise a CPO to accept a deal on a handshake, or a verbal agreement over coffee. On the other hand, how you feel during that first encounter is important. You may not have the luxury of a sit-down meeting. They may want protection two hours from now and be three hours away. If that happens, don't throw your standard paperwork out the window. Tell them that you'll send over the agreement the following day, and then follow through to get it signed.

But how do you protect yourself on that first day? You can record the call and read off your list of standard disclaimers (or have your office manager do it).

Always negotiate from a position of power. What this means is that you have already determined exactly what the client needs and wants. You have properly profiled your client. You know what is in their "thought bubble." You know where they are financially and what their budget is.

Fortunately, not all deals are last-minute. You'll often have weeks or months to negotiate before the final sign-off. Handlers for politicians and celebrities can usually give you plenty of lead time, because their events are planned months in advance. The same is true of event security.

If you have bought a home or invested in real estate, you will have had experience with the negotiation process that occurs in the weeks before you sign a contract.

For big deals, you may even need to fly to meet your clients (a good way to show urgency). Always have an organized paper trail of emails, notes, etc. from each phone conference or other communication in your "negotiation kit" and be completely familiar with what you have. Make sure your thoughts and motives leading to the agreement can be verbally backed up as you negotiate. Study the contract and terms of the agreement or scope of services fully. Be prepared.

If this is something new to you—negotiating, talking, explaining and increasing your value—then bring a more experienced friend to the meeting. Find a mentor. Sit in and listen to the "buzzwords" of the negotiations. Is it a local EP job where minor points of wording have to be ironed out, or is it a federal case that will need signatures of judges, attorneys, companies, or agencies? Just imagine the different experience during negotiations. And that's what you need. Experience. The more time you spend in front of people—asking for a better deal, promoting solutions, proposing counter-offers—the more comfortable and confident you will be.

Make sure you know who the ultimate decision maker is and that they are in the loop so that you don't show up and have to resell the entire agreement.

When negotiating a contract, hold your cards close to your chest. Don't let them know everything in your mind. Always leave wiggle room. One approach is to insist on provisions you can actually do without. When you get push-back, you can now "cave in" and barter away things that aren't important to you while keeping the important points (including your price) intact.

One of the best factors in negotiating a contract is your attitude. Are you a positive, "can do" type of person? If you demonstrate that you can make this executive protection detail happen and handle the safety of the client(s), you are earning their trust. And believe me, a large proportion of contracts signed are because of trust! The power of your positive energy will work in your favor, especially if you are operating with an abundance of customer service. I honestly enjoy negotiating deals and it helps me better understand what I am getting myself into.

More Tips on the Negotiating Process

Relax. Breathe. Slow down and read each line. To this day, no matter what agreement I sign, I literally read every word. Out of all of the contracts I have signed in over 20 years, 90% of the contracts have had edits and deletions. If someone is trying to rush you, that is a bright red flag.

Get legal advice. I try to always have my attorneys read anything I sign that is a major deal. However, be careful when selecting an attorney. Find one who is aggressive and can take your calls. If an attorney is too busy to take your calls or return calls, move on. You also don't want a simple task to take months and months of back and forth phone calls and emails. So always ask an attorney the equivalent of, "When does this end?" In other words, ask them for a realistic timeline that you can depend on, and hold them to it. Nudge them if you have to, but if their delays start costing you business, find someone else.

Weigh the risk vs. the reward. How much is there to gain and lose? Is the reward worth the risks, the threats you will be dealing with? What about legal liabilities? Think about that from a monetary point of view. You want your money to remain YOUR money. You don't want to be in a situation where the risk is too high, because even if you win in court, you lose at the bank.

Be understanding. In order to be understanding of your client's needs and wants, you actually need to know their needs and wants. Once you know this vital information you now can negotiate the contract from a point of strength. Use their words to specify and strengthen your services.

Have a 30-day-out clause. It is essential that you include a 30-day-out clause for a positive outcome if problems arise that can't be resolved. For either party, if we're not happy, instead of cutting each other off at the ankles, we just say we will have a "30-day-out" clause. Now, within that 30-day clause, either of us can cancel the agreement; but what we try to do is find a solution to keep the agreement going. So the clause is out of respect for both parties: me and the client. If they are absolutely not happy with me, then I as a professional wouldn't want to take their money. I would want to fix the problem. Same thing in reverse. If these clients aren't listening to me or taking my professional advice, recommendations, or requests, and I know that there is something that is going to be putting us in jeopardy, then I say, maybe you should start looking for a different company, and I will give you 30 days to do that, because you are not following my recommendations. In that case, I give them 30 days to fix the problem. So it is just a respectful way of two parties bowing out. But it gives you 30 days for either side to try and fix and overcome problems, so you don't have to lose the agreement.

Define limitations of service. Your contract, or agreement, defines the scope and limitations of services promised. The agreement must limit your liability, because there's only so much you can guarantee. If you're only guarding the protectee within a building, specify: "This protection does not extend to adjacent property or sidewalks."

Your agreement needs to include a statement that you will abide by the laws of the jurisdiction the detail will be conducted in. Any conflict between the law and the client's instructions will be settled in favor of the law.

Divide the contract up. Some agreements fall apart because some attorneys take an "all or nothing" approach, in which the other party must agree to all of their terms in order to move forward. This is why it is important to take sections of the contract and agree to those sections verbally or with initials. For example, it is not uncommon to ask for a "Proof of Funds" letter. By considering the contract in sections and getting "yes" answers to portions, you will eventually arrive at a completed contract.

Get the Yes! Look ahead and understand the real level of interest, the true threat, and any red flags that may impede the signing of this contract. *Come with true contingencies for each point. Generate options, not opposition.* Create an environment within the negotiation where problems are solved with competence, intelligence and swiftness. Offset, defuse, and redirect conflicts to the objectives and solutions.

Who's in control? If you want to be in control of the negotiations, it is imperative to have the decision maker in the room or on the phone. If you are asking the questions, then you can decide which topics will be discussed. If someone keeps trying to turn it around where they aren't answering your questions but only asks you questions, completely change the entire subject. If you change the entire topic, you are indirectly saying NO. Then go back to asking the questions you want answered. For example, let's say that for some reason you simply cannot gain the ground you need, and need to take another approach that requires some research. Again, change the entire topic and offer a summation of the meeting and where it stands, to be drafted up and signed by both parties as to the meeting minutes. At that time, the meeting should be recessed.

Communicate. Don't be afraid to ask questions. The key word here is "ASK." This is, first of all, how to stay in control of conversations when speaking to people. If for some reason the other party is taking a tough position on certain key issues, ask: Why? Why are those issues of such importance? Once you have done this, you will have done three things. One, you will have gotten control of the conversation/meeting. Two, both parties will fully understand the importance of their issues. Three, now you will have gotten inside their bubble. Sell them what they just stressed to you. By this time their emotions should be engaged and you can close the deal, and all because you asked, "Why?"

Deal with facts. When I enter into negotiations, I separate my professional thinking from my personal thoughts. I never violate my moral compass, and my clients appreciate that. Effective negotiators are able to detach business from personal preferences, facts from feelings. Basically, if it makes sense factually, then the dollars will make sense. This is business, not personal.

Understand who you are dealing with. You want to find out more about the person you are talking to, and not alienate them in the process. Steer clear of expressions that make it sound personal, such as "I know," "I think," "I want." Role-play this if you need to until it begins to come naturally. Instead, say, "I understand." That is very, very comforting.

You can gain insight by listening. He might say, "I see things are going to be moving in this direction." He's a visual person. If she speaks in terms of "I feel," then she is more of a physical person. "I feel we are going to be moving in this direction." He's a hands-on person. If the person says, "I sense that…," she is forward thinking, looking into the future.

I say, "I understand what you are saying." And then I ask a question to get more information. "Can you expand on that? Why is it that you are having those thoughts? Why is it that you believe that?" I let them keep talking and I keep listening, without interrupting, so I can better pinpoint who they are—again, profiling. I am learning the facts, not influenced by the opinions, the fears, the negativity. I am sorting and rearranging: I don't need that, I don't need this. I just move it away. I never take it off the table, I just keep moving the important things back to the center.

These are all things that you have to understand when you are talking to different people. It is the same thing as when I was dealing with children, teaching them martial arts. I did not expect them to match my mentality and speak to me at my level. I had to change my mentality and explain to them in a way that they could understand. It's the same thing in this industry. If a person is not an expert in executive protection, I can't expect them to come up to my level of expertise and understand what I am seeing, because they are not there. It is empty space to them. So I have to meet them at their level and educate them enough to understand where I'm at on my level.

Keep calm and close the deal. At this point, having done your best to pre-frame the client, discovered what's inside their mental bubble and presented a draft of the contract for signature, half the things you wrote may go right out the window. Stay calm. If you don't understand something, ask for an explanation and get clarity. Everything down the road is renegotiable if you've built that flexibility into the terms.

Negotiate with Confidence. Confidence means knowing you're right and knowing you can hold your position. You don't yield if you are right. You will concede a point if it's a gray area.

You want to arrive at a win-win, not a win-lose. That means you're not opponents, but collaborators in this deal. If it's viewed that way by both sides, the process will always go smoothly.

Are there multiple decision makers? Will the deal be discussed with a spouse who doesn't know you or is unsympathetic to you? Don't set up anything where they could shoot you down. Attorneys will pounce on anything that's open to interpretation, so don't leave those openings.

Are you up against someone who wants to win at your expense? In that case, prepare to hold the line, but set up some bargaining chips that you're fully prepared to concede—and dole them out sparingly.

11

Management

What Are the Hallmarks of a Professional?

I lead by example and represent the company in a way that we keep growing. That means I also have expectations of my team members to maintain the same level of integrity that I expect of myself. I'm very friendly, and I don't like to micromanage people, because if I'm micromanaging you, now I'm doing it and I don't need you; I'll do it myself. I expect us to be adults, where I can give a team member instructions and get what I expect—but I also will inspect what I expect.

I prefer to look at my team from the viewpoint that they work *with* me, rather than *for* me, because I will put on the boots, the shirt, and the gun, and do the same post that they're doing. In fact, every post that we have, I've done, in the security field.

Leading a team means being able to think outside the box, think through all the contingencies of a situation, and maintain full focus on what you're doing and why you're doing it—without getting into tunnel vision. All that is part of training, and that applies to the business side of executive protection, as well as the security detail.

A good boss is decisive. If something goes wrong, he takes effective action. Once things are back under control, he brings everyone up to speed on what happened and why. All this comes from his certainty about the technology of bodyguarding and the technology of management. Nobody is left wondering where they stand.

Anyone can call himself a professional. But what do his actions demonstrate? When leading a team, is he being the team lead, or just one of the guys? How seriously does he take his duties? There's no down time on a detail. If you let the slow times lull you into thinking there's no danger, that's the danger. Life throws a punch as soon as you let your guard down.

Problem Solver

From either the team lead or CEO viewpoint, I have to:

- Lead by example.
- Step in and handle any position that goes vacant for any reason, temporarily or otherwise.
- Train new or experienced CPOs to fine-tune their performance.
- Clarify how things are done according to their playbook.
- Correct mistakes.
- Market my company.
- Manage my team.
- Handle all legal aspects with my attorney and accountant.
- All while still managing my multiple companies and real estate portfolio.

You have to be able to picture the detail in your mind, before deployment and throughout the process. You have to know at any time what each position is supposed to be doing. The guys on the ground know how to close a gap if a teammate falls out, but the guy in command has to make sure it happens *now-now-now*.

If you have to swap someone out, you do it with a minimum of ruffled feathers.

Can you keep a cool head under fire? A leader has to. Go ahead and accept a few challenges that stretch your comfort zone a little. Patch up the goofs as they happen and note policy changes you'll need to make so it doesn't happen again.

Along the way, you'll figure out what you're really made of.

Can you switch fluidly between the CPO mindset and the CEO mindset? Can you solve problems creatively in the moment, gamble on being right, and be right most of the time? You'll make it. Especially since you're still reading this book.

Quality Control

I do a lot of random post checks. I ask them to show me how they work. What is on their activity report? What are they doing in their downtime? What can I suggest to them to keep active during downtime? The first two rules that I live by are, "Do not sit in your car or you will go to sleep," and "Stay off your phone." If people cannot follow these two simple rules, they are not part of my team.

What I expect from my guys is true professionalism. I want them to work as if they owned the company. If people don't work with you as if they want to own a company one day, there really is no incentive for them to maintain a high work ethic.

With that being said, you always have to inspire them, motivate them, be on their page. You have to learn what motivates them, what keeps them driven. Is it family? Is it school? Is it education? What part of them will inspire them to work harder, to be more loyal, and to have a stronger work ethic than others?

Constant Alertness

As a CPO, but even more so as a team lead, I'm constantly alert to whatever is happening within the perimeter of my vision. If nothing is changing, I'm capturing more information about my surroundings, noting dangers and opportunities. I can do this while appearing to be 100% absorbed in the conversation I'm having.

Recently I was sitting at the café in Barnes & Noble with my editor, going over this book. An older gentleman cut into our conversation wanting to offer some expert advice about whatever we might be working on. We politely declined, and a few minutes later he lifted the baseball cap off another customer's table and walked around wearing it. Entertaining himself. Then he put it back. I also observed that the ceiling was missing a few acoustic panels, probably due to water damage from a recent hurricane. Whether on a detail or just hanging out, I'm always alert to my surroundings.

Maintaining Your Image

It's very important to keep in mind that you don't ever want to put out a bad image. You want to be professional at all times because wherever your name goes, so does your reputation. You always want your name to stay on top.

When you're on a detail, the public will not really see what you are doing unless you are creating a hard target. However, if the client wants to be known for his hard security, then people around you will see you and make a decision based on how you act in that role.

Perception is reality. How you interact with the public while off duty should not be much different than how you act in public when on a detail.

How you act in public is part of your brand, whether on detail or not. If I'm enjoying a night out, I don't drop my public persona. Some guys don't remember what they did the night before. Is that what you want for a leader? I didn't think so.

Fielding an Effective Team

Executive protection teams are often put together on short notice. This means you need a network of subcontractors you can depend on, who won't choke under pressure—and you know they don't because you've worked with them. That's the ideal. If you haven't worked with them, chances are you know somebody who has.

If you've been a team lead, you know the motions your team will go through on a detail.

To establish that team, you need to assess these basic factors:

- What specialties must be represented on the team?
- How many CPOs do we need?
- Does the client agree to pay for that many?
- What is the threat?
- What are the risks?
- Terms and conditions?
- Length of the detail?
- Now vs. later?
- Short term vs. long term?

My network includes a lot of my students. (I don't call them "former students" because they are always welcome to redo a class at no charge, any number of times. We never stop learning—I'm no exception.) All my guys and gals are great CPOs, and a lot of them are great team leads as well. These are CPOs I know personally, so I know their capabilities. Some live close, some a few hours away, some in different states or abroad. Many are in the islands of the Caribbean.

If I put someone in charge in another state and a negotiating situation comes up, I'll have to assess what I know about their skills as a negotiator. If I sense it's a weakness, I'll do the deal-making for them, even if there's nothing in it for me immediately. Setting guys up to win will come back around—and so will the opposite.

In this business, connections are king. I keep repeating this because it is so, so key to a successful business.

The one thing that never changes is that everything changes. Just when everyone is in place and ready to go, the client changes destinations, changes the times, adds more people to the party, or pulls out altogether. The team lead who can roll with the punches will succeed. The guy with tunnel vision, zeroed in obsessively on that one role, location, and position, will find things a bit rough until he lightens up a little.

Team Members and Physical Fitness

When you are in a bad situation, and you don't have a weapon, you find whatever you can to defend yourself. It is the same thing when you put a team together. You want the best, most highly qualified people, but I can use people who aren't as physically strong as me.

I will always bring someone on the team who can help me do site surveillance, do background checks, do covert things for me, but not put them in harm's way.

I'll give you an example. Once I had a person on my team who didn't look the part. Other team members expressed displeasure. I told them I understood their position, but I was responsible for them being on the team, so they could get more experience. They didn't realize that this person was going through chemotherapy.

Coaching Your Team

What do you do when you are in the field working with people, and someone makes a mistake. This situation will inevitably happen and you need to become adept at handling it. The thing to do is pick them up, not put them down. The worst thing you can do is slash someone's self-esteem. However good they are, if you trash them, they'll trash themselves ten times as bad. With that standard in mind, here are my favorite coaching tips that I have learned over the years.

PCP – Praise, Correct, Praise

Good workers become great workers through the cycle of "praise, correct, praise," a proven successful coaching technique. They'll work a lot harder to be validated than to avoid being invalidated. If you have to correct someone, take them aside to do it. Embarrassment before one's peers is a terrible morale killer.

Not everyone has the skills and stamina that you do, but you can find out what's great about them and cultivate that. You have to have their buy-in as team players. If they're committed to the success of the detail, they'll make good choices and make you look good. If they fall short of that standard, you must correct them—privately. Public humiliation won't make them tougher, just resentful. Don't copy your drill instructor.

Adjust Your Approach to Your Client

When I had weekly meetings with my staff at my martial arts school, I would have the following conversation.

"Who are the problem kids?" (It would pretty much be the same names cropping up.)

"Will they show up with the same problems at their next lesson?" (Without a doubt.)

"Then don't be surprised or frustrated when they do. Control what you can control. You didn't raise them, you can't control their home environment, but you *can* deliver a standard lesson, and that is expected of you every time. Parents will pay for that. They won't pay for excuses."

It is similar with executive protection. Some clients have their own little quirks. They may be anxious and unable to focus on your questions. So, the discovery process for a detail changes under these circumstances. You can't change this client's state of mind, so you have to adjust your own approach.

Play to Your CPOs' Strengths

At any given time, I have thirty to forty CPOs working directly under my license, and sometimes it grows to over a hundred. These aren't necessarily all-star teams or "dream teams." But I can bring out the best in them by playing to their strengths and drilling them as a unit. Any pro team can beat an all-star team because they know the playbook and they make each other better.

When I have "B" or "C" level people working for me, I coach them. I teach them. As long as they will put in the honest effort, I help them. When I get "A" level talent, I help them too. Maybe they need help with insurance coverage, my procurement of clients, or my network. After a few details they may want to strike off on their own, and I'll help with that too. It comes back to me eventually.

The One-Minute Manager

How to be an effective manager is covered in a book that is one of my personal favorites: *The One Minute Manager* by Kenneth Blanchard and Spencer Johnson. I like it because it's easy to read and offers practical advice, not empty theories.

The book tells the story of a young man's search for an effective manager, one he would like to work for. He's had bosses before, but all of them fell short of his seemingly simple requirements.

This young man describes the two types of managers he has personally encountered.

The first type is the slave driver who cares only about the bottom line and is indifferent to the welfare of his staff. The second type is the manager who tries to be popular and doesn't demand enough. Knowing this, the young man wonders if he will ever meet someone who combines the good points of both approaches.

In his search, the young man meets some "autocratic" managers who are only concerned about the results. Yet the results ultimately suffer from the dissatisfaction of personnel who aren't empowered to make their own decisions.

He also meets "democratic" managers who are concerned only about what "the people" want. The problem here is that popular decisions are very often bad decisions. There are a thousand wrong choices in any given situation, and very few right ones. Making consistently good decisions requires not only exceptionally good judgment; it also requires knowing all the data and understanding all the viewpoints—data that is only available from a top-level view.

If a leader gives up the leadership viewpoint and runs things from the viewpoint of "one of the people," this is like the pilot sitting down in a passenger seat. Who's flying the thing?

Under a "democratic" manager, employees gain in the short term, but in the long term they bleed the organization dry. Organizations have to make money before they can spend it. Payroll comes out of cash flow, not out of some mysterious vault.

He hears that such a manager exists—not halfway across the globe, but in a neighboring town. This manager is eager to share his secrets, because they shouldn't be secrets—the success of other managers isn't a threat to him.

Running your organization is a role you can't abandon. It is also vital that your staff know their roles and don't try to overstep their place in your company. Oftentimes, I see people trip themselves up with unrealistic expectations. They self-promote and imagine that they're bigger than the true picture. Such workers will end up being replaced by somebody better, faster, smarter. If you drive that point home, you will never lose your company, or lose staff. But if you manage the expectations of your staff, they will stay within the healthy bounds of your company.

One-Minute Self Coaching

The One-Minute Manager helps you coach your team, but you can use it to coach yourself. You can get your time management down to the minute: "At this minute, what am I doing?" And if you constantly manage yourself in your mind with a one-minute manager, it's as easy as saying, "If there's time to lean, there's time to clean."

If you're a professional, and you have high expectations of yourself and your team, then every minute has to be accounted for. As a one-minute manager, you should always be asking yourself, "At this minute, what am I doing to grow the company, maintain the company, and make sure that it is on a strong foundation? At this minute, what am I doing to brand myself, market myself? At this minute, what am I doing to get a new client?"

If you're leading the team, you have to ask yourself, at this minute where is my team? Where are we going to be? Where are we going to go? At this very minute, what is the next move?

If you are on the team, your minute is, where is my left, where is my right, where is my forward? If you are in business, and you're trying to grow the business, at this very minute, you are asking yourself, what am I doing? Am I on Facebook, on social media, am I texting? Or am I actually doing something productive? So the one-minute thinking is, what am I doing this very minute to either protect the client, get a new sale, sign a new agreement, etc.?

One Minute Goal Setting

You set goals and summarize them in a form that can be read in one minute. One-minute goal-setting is about being aware of what is expected from the beginning. A goal is named; performance standards are set; these things are stated on a single sheet of paper.

One-minute goals work because they're measurable. A player on the field knows whether he scored or not. Does a guard on a detail know whether his work is making the client happy or is about to get him fired? If he's uncertain about these things, it will affect his performance. If the goals for the detail have been written down on one sheet, are understood and agreed on, the team will work cohesively to get those goals met.

This ties right into the need for statistics that measure progress toward small goals as well as large ones. It also ties into the "M" of our "SMART goals" discussed earlier in the section on Goal Setting: goals should be Measurable.

One-Minute Praisings

After the one-minute goal setting, the second step in one-minute management is to catch people doing something right. This is when the one-minute praisings are given. One-minute praisings are so called because it hardly takes a minute for you to tell someone what is great about their work and how it makes you feel. This is positive reinforcement: whatever they did right, they'll want to keep doing it.

The key to one-minute praisings is to deliver them on the spot, or as soon as convenient thereafter.

Good personnel are always improving their game by learning new skills and new viewpoints. They learn quicker if positive feedback is available, so teach this to your field managers as well.

One-minute praisings show that you are genuinely interested in your people and care for them and their success. One-minute praisings aim at catching people "doing something right" rather than catching them "doing something wrong" like the autocratic managers (dictators) tend to do. This fits well in the model of PCP—Praise, Correct, Praise.

If you only correct, you smother initiative. People who are the brunt of criticism without praise may reduce their activity so they don't make a mistake. You want them to be motivated about their positions, constantly promoting customer service and your brand.

If you've been in the military, you know all about autocratic managers, because it's built into the culture. Nobody wants a democratic military, for obvious reasons. Yet they could still "praise, correct, praise" without undermining discipline, and get much better results. Agree or disagree?

One-Minute Reprimands

One-minute reprimands are given as soon as an employee does something wrong, or as soon as you know about it. In a hierarchy, you won't necessarily be right there when it happens. So your field managers have to acquire this skill as well. You want to maintain the chain of command as much as possible, so you apply one-minute reprimands to your immediate juniors and they do it with theirs.

The one-minute reprimand has two parts. The first half includes telling the people what they did wrong, how you feel about it and then let it sink in with a few seconds of uncomfortable silence. Then in the second half you tell the people how much you think they are capable of and how much you value them.

One important aspect of one-minute reprimands is that it criticizes the work, not the doer. The employee must not feel personally attacked. He or she is not being blamed as a person; only his work is accused of not being up to standard. And once you've made that understood, it's over.

Some people make this difficult. The guy who walks around with a chip on his shoulder is likely to take it personally anyway. This is where the "praise" component of Praise-Correct-Praise (PCP) can save the day. But if that doesn't work, you have a hard case on your hands, not a team member, and you have to act accordingly.

One-minute reprimands are highly effective because the feedback is immediate, unlike the annual reviews where you are charged for faults committed several weeks or months ago. Being scolded for a mistake you made seven or eight months back would certainly make you uncomfortable, but it wouldn't improve your performance. On the other hand, if you are being scolded for a mistake you made yesterday, you can remember the circumstances (and set the record straight if needed). If a mistake is pointed out as soon as it is made, it can easily be corrected. Generalities such as "You always do this," or "You never do that," have no place in corrections, and are bound to cause upsets. Be specific.

12

Secure and Grow Your Wealth

Ultimately, your goal is to be successful. Visualize it, plan for it, don't just hope for it. That plan should include protecting your assets and limiting your liabilities. You can't always go backwards and protect yourself once you hit the big time. You need to plan for it and put protective measures in place before you become successful, so that once you do, your affairs are in order. Consult with a business attorney and an accountant. It's time and money well spent to ensure you structure your business in the way that will benefit and protect you the most.

You have to be willing to invest in yourself if you expect others to invest in you. This sometimes takes sacrifice, but most importantly, requires you to live within your means.

"I'm broke." No you're not. Maybe your cash flow is negative, maybe you're spending 10% more than you make, like the typical American household. So cut back your spending by 20%.

Where are you throwing money away? If you can cut out cigarettes, that's more than $2000 a year for a pack-a-day habit. Have everybody in the family who is spending money come up with one way they can stop throwing away money. Make that Starbucks trip a special occasion, not an automatic daily ritual. This is one where you definitely have to lead by example.

When you're working for yourself, write yourself a regular paycheck and let any surplus accumulate in the bank to see you through lean times. If you tend to blow all your money as soon as you have some, consider having someone else manage your money.

Read *The Richest Man in Babylon*. It talks about saving 10% of your money no matter what. I have a small river house. Every time I go there, I'll put in a few dollars in a money can. I go up, I go hunting, work on the land,

and I always put a little bit of money into that can. Always have a reserve of money, so that you can move, fast. Opportunity comes in the blink of an eye.

I lived within or below my means so I could continue to invest in myself, in my businesses, in the people around me. Keep reinvesting the surplus in your company. Don't go out and waste it. I work with the money that is in hand; I never look at the money that is put away for savings, except in the event of a true emergency. By spending a little money reinforcing the things that make your business different and great, your unique value proposition will become stronger and stronger.

I personally recommend investing 20% of your income rather than 10%. Here are some vehicles I have chosen to invest in and expand my own financial portfolio:

- real estate rentals
- stocks (I invested in a bank as a stock holder.)
- Roth IRAs (retirement account)
- land (raw land for future investments)
- my executive protection school (my bodyguard classes, separate from my security company)
- new businesses (any new opportunity for positive cash flow—car wash, laundry mat)
- my security company (International EP LLC—static security, event security, etc.)
- my FPL (Federal Firearm License)—I buy and sell guns legally with a license.
- IEP Vet Fund.org to help soldiers and veterans
- Book sales
- Tactical Gear (sales of supplies)

One thing you need to think about when planning your future finances is that you may want to help to ensure your parents are taken care of. If you're still young, you probably don't have dependent parents and probably aren't thinking this far ahead. Old age is usually not very real to young people unless they are fully involved with their elderly grandparents. It's something to be aware of, however: when your parents get into their late sixties and beyond, they are going to slow down and have more frequent physical problems. At some point they may need a caregiver. Make sure they are thinking ahead and have something planned besides just Social Security.

The first conversation on the subject can be tough, because you have to break out of your customary role of being the "kid" and become the trusted advisor. Make sure they have good insurance coverage and are paying into a retirement plan. The money's not for you: it is for making sure you don't suddenly have heavy financial burdens at the point that you're ready to start thinking about retirement yourself.

13

Heart-to-Heart, Me to You

I wrote this book because I want you to succeed. With that in mind, I want to end this book with a heart-to-heart coaching session, me to you.

Be Coachable

One of the keys to success is to be coachable. If you are not coachable, then that means you are untrainable. If you are untrainable, then you are stuck in your own ways. The reason why I became a world champion, the reason I became a success in business, the reason I became an author, is because I listened to people who were experts. I was coachable. I did not interrupt and say, "No, no, no, this is how you do it." I would shut up and listen.

So you have to be coachable. When he's in the ring, a boxer is on his own, but as soon as he sits down between rounds, he'd better listen to his trainer.

In my business, if my director of operations points out something I've overlooked, I have to be coachable. It could be really important. Same thing in the field. If I see something that you don't see, and I point it out, don't immediately cut me off and say, "I got it." No, no, no, no! Be coachable.

Be coachable in anything you do. It means stop and listen. Think about it. Digest it in your mind. Come into the class and let me teach you. When people follow my instructions and my blueprint, they are successful. They need to listen, understand what I am saying or get it clarified, take notes, and practice the motions. If I say to them, "Do x, y and z, follow through, and you're going to have success," I mean exactly that.

At what level? I don't know. Nobody knows that. You want to set the bar as high as you can, but you don't want to set yourself up for failure.

When I say that people who follow my blueprint are successful, they are successful on their own terms and by their own standards. My student Deo, in Aruba, is extremely successful with his company now. Brent with his company in Trinidad and Tobago is very successful now. Aaron French was my student. He's now director of my company. I brought him aboard. You can read Deo's and Brent's success stories in the appendices of this book. These people were coachable. Even though they were highly trained, I retrained them, taught them different businesses. We were like-minded people. And we were a brotherhood, a family.

Once I had someone call me and say, "Why didn't my husband find a job?"

I asked if her husband had followed the few simple principles I always teach the class.

"Did he get on my Facebook page?"

"No."

"Well, did he get on my LinkedIn page?"

"No."

"Did he make any business cards?"

"No."

"Has he done anything to try and brand himself?"

"No."

"Has he gone to any sort of meetings to introduce himself?"

"No."

I said, "Well, how is he supposed to be successful? Did you put him in the closet? If he didn't follow the simple keys to success that were laid out in front of him, how would you ever expect him to be successful?"

Success is not going to fall into your lap. You have to go out and take these steps. Go out and hustle. Be first in line. Be the first one at the negotiating table and the last one to sign. If you are the first one at the table, you are the first one to understand what is going on. Be the last one to sign, so you can see what is going on. Be the last one to talk. That way you can't get trapped into anything. Keep your mouth shut and listen. And then you have the last say, because you know what everybody else is thinking.

Have an open mind and think for yourself while being coachable. That is what leads to victory.

I have been very blessed to have taught many people and made a difference in their lives. They have become more secure financially, redeveloped their character to become a better person overall, and gotten better at the jobs they have now. One thing that I strive to do is not just teach them about EP, but teach them about life. I try to also teach them that you don't know what other people are going through. You don't know the hardships that they are thinking about. Is their mom sick? Is their dad okay? Is their dad in the hospital? These are all things that you may not know, because people tend to keep these difficulties to themselves.

Exhaust All Avenues

Many times people call me and tell me they want to do executive protection. I ask them about their background. I ask them if they are ex-military, ex-police officer, do they have any experience in the past, any martial arts experience. The next follow up question is, what books have you read on business, what books have you read on executive protection, what books have you read about being a CEO while working in the field as a CPO? Because I want to understand their level of enthusiasm and commitment.

I ask, "Have you exhausted everything to achieve what you want? Have you read everything—every journal, every blog, every book, every magazine? Have you talked to people about the combinations and approaches that you wish to take to get to the next level in a company?

Have you researched possibilities that nobody knew about? Is there another company out there that has done the same task that you are attempting to do? Have you talked to people in other industries or in other companies similar to yours and asked them questions, to understand their tactics or their ways of marketing their skills, and what makes them different? If they are better than you, then why are they better than you?" These are the sorts of things you should be pursuing exhaustively to get to the next level.

People will say, I want to be a bodyguard. Okay. What do you know about it? The first thing I say in class now is, "If you have a living will and everything prepared for your death, raise your hand." Now I have their attention. People don't think of the danger. They look at the glamour. They think of the Kardashians, and situations like that. That is unrealistic for people like us, because celebrities are going to hire Secret Service, FBI. Or they will hire just a big thug who has no mental capability of doing it, whose longevity is very limited. But the former FBI or Secret Service guys who put teams together, their longevity is great because they have a business. I want my students setting their sights on owning a business, not just working for one.

So that's how you plan for longevity, whether in business, training, or networking. Exhaust every resource of knowledge, all avenues, about becoming a bodyguard, to understand what a bodyguard does, to understand what a bodyguard has to go through, to understand what you have to do to succeed in business. Have you read everything? Or are you just going to come and take a three-day class and think you are going to be a millionaire overnight?

So when I ask them if they have exhausted everything, this is when I start to open up their eyes, and open up their mind to reality. It takes hard work, dedication and education to become successful, not just in executive protection, but in anything that you do.

Forever Forward

Turn your goals and visions into reality. But you have to work at it daily. Either you are all in or you are all out. You have to take the same approach in business as you do in a fight. Keep moving forward. Take the next step. Forever forward. Keep learning, keep moving, keep your ambitions high. You have to train your mind and dedicate your time to the goals that you want to achieve.

If you don't make the time to achieve your goals, to see your vision come true, to watch yourself cross the finish line, then you have no finish line to cross.

If you truly want to be successful in anything that you do, dedicate yourself to it. If you do anything halfheartedly, you are wasting your time and my time and your money. Constantly write down your goals and constantly strive to achieve them: daily, weekly, monthly, yearly. Have a five-year plan and a ten-year plan.

Being a dreamer is one thing, but don't forget: we only get things done when we are awake. So while you're awake, stop dreaming, and start doing whatever it is that you need to do to accomplish your goals. Start off with small steps, but have a grand goal in mind. Set your sights on it and follow through. I have said this many times before: the fortune is in the follow-up and follow-through.

What can be done today can be done now. What can be done tomorrow can be done today.

There is a lot of room at the top because most people bow out once it gets a little rocky. Success is not easy. Success is hard work and constant dedication to becoming and achieving whatever your vision is.

Don't forget that executive protection has limited individual longevity. After that you can do consulting. Our bodies get tired. We get weaker, but our minds must be sharp. We must always prepare for the future. By that point, you should have established multiple avenues of income.

Always try to save as much money as you can and invest into something that is going to benefit you in the future. Just as you multitask in executive protection, you also have to multitask in business. In other words, reinvest the money in yourself, and then reinvest the money in something else, because we can't do this forever. That's why I have over 20 rental income properties. I invest in real estate.

Life is short. So run as fast as you can for as long as you can.

One day you will realize you cannot run as fast as you once could. Things slow down in the end. It is at that time that your hard work and dedication to your business should pay off.

You should work hard for your money in the beginning, and let your money work hard for you in the end.

Each and every day you will face challenges. But forever forward. Always move forward, no matter how small a step it is. Always move the ball forward. Always be climbing toward the top of the mountain.

And if you are not leading, then follow a strong leader. Too many people wander around following people who just talk about things. Follow somebody who puts things into motion. Follow somebody who follows through instead of talking about what they're going to do. They follow through with actions.

How to Deal With Failures and Setbacks

Just remember, you never lose if you learn from failure. There always will be some good that comes out of failures or setbacks. Don't get down on yourself, and don't beat yourself up. Lift yourself up. If things are going bad, there's going to be a lesson that comes out of it.

If you didn't get the contract you wanted, so be it. That will give you time to find a bigger contract. You didn't get the client you wanted? So be it. Who got them? Why? You will have gained more experience to get a better client. Learn from it. What did he do better than you? Find a solution to it. Don't get frustrated. Just look at the issue and determine what there is to learn from it. Take that step back and find something that you can learn from it, and bring it back to your team, to yourself, to your mind, and build on it.

You are not failing if you are learning. You are not losing if you are learning.

Too many times, when people are successful, they champion themselves. But you should champion the people who helped you get there. When you fail at something, you should accept it and own it. Failure is a brutal teacher, but it teaches lessons you cannot forget.

When things go wrong, you have to own it. When things go well, you pass the credit along.

You have to take ownership when things don't go your way. Don't blame other people when you are the one in charge. There is no excuse to put the blame on anyone else if you are leader, and manager and CEO. Everything is in your hands. When things are going well, give credit where it's due. When things are going bad, you are the only one to blame.

Afterwards, we implement things, redesign things, rewrite things, review things so that it doesn't happen again, so that you can never be wrong again in that situation. When things go wrong, we have to understand what we did wrong. When you take ownership of the problem or situation that went wrong, then you have the solutions. Don't pass it off to somebody else, or else nothing gets solved, and nothing gets improved.

Don't be afraid of failure. Don't run from it. Run towards it.

The only way to overcome any challenges that you face is to take the next step. Every day, no matter what is going on around you, get up and start moving toward your goal.

You've lived your life for this moment. Now step forward into it.

Be aggressive toward your goals, but not overbearing when negotiating agreements or contracts. Don't be afraid of pushing to make the deal. There's only one way to find out if you're going to get the next contract, and that is to confront that person or that company. That way you can flush out the objections. After that, you will learn more for the next deal. But you have to take that next step.

It is not easy to get the next contract, so what you have to do is control what you can control. You have to remain vigilant to what is happening in the industry. You have to always stay aggressive and maintain discipline, so that when you do get that next contract or opportunity, it will be because you have already out-thought your competition, and you can take control of the situation.

Analyze the industry. Analyze your competition. You have to be prepared for what is coming, and what your response is going to be. Read what your competitors post on social media. Read threat analysis reports. You don't know exactly what the markets are going to do for the next trend or bubble.

Find out what you can. Have a secondary plan to execute if you have to. But you have to maintain discipline to make this work. A lot of businesses are unpredictable. When there is chaos, you can only control yourself. You have to outthink the chaos and the competition.

Always analyze the competition and the business around you and strive to be three steps ahead of them. You may not know what the competition is doing to stop you from getting the next contract or stop you from getting the next client. Be a chameleon-like business so they don't know what your next move is going to be. Don't let people know your next step. Again, control your own thoughts and maintain your daily discipline to constantly keep moving forward.

You have to brand yourself to leverage people—to influence them for an outcome in your favor. But it has to be authentic. You have to be you. You have to be yourself in business. You cannot be fake or people will see right through you. Be yourself, and be honest. If you have branded yourself properly, when you walk in that room, they know who you are already. When you make your move, you have already won the hearts of half of the people in the room.

If your business goals and values are aligned with your moral compass, you will be successful, because then you will be authentic. Too many people try to cheat the competition, and cheat this and cheat that. It's not authentic and that's not a happy life. Be real. That's it.

Godspeed

Congratulations on completing this book, and Godspeed. Always be safe in what you are doing. Don't build a false sense of security. Go out there and hustle. Go out there and win the industry. Own it.

Be aggressive. Be humble. Be kind. Lift people up. Don't put people down. Always help the weak. The people who are strong, stand next to them. The people who are weak, bring them next to you. Always empower the people around you. I think the society and the community and the world would be a lot better if the people who had a higher position or more powerful position lifted people up instead of stepping on them to get to the top.

If you have any questions, you can email me directly at lenny@ internationalep.com. Always check back with us for new, upcoming classes and new information about details coming up.

Appendix I

Glossary

This will be a much shorter glossary than the one found in *Bodyguard Myth*. If you want a more comprehensive glossary of the nuts and bolts of executive protection, please refer to that book.

Advance

Same as **Advance team**.

Advance team

The team (or, loosely, an individual) that scouts and clears routes and destinations for the detail. This includes meeting with and pre-framing the hotel manager, the convention organizer, the handler or executive assistant who made the arrangements for the client's arrival.

Determines everything that needs to be known in advance. Where the hotel is for the team, what's surrounding it, where the roads are, what times of the day they are busier, less busy, traffic, high traffic, low traffic, construction, no construction. Routes from point A to point B, exactly how long it's going to take at various times. The Advance Team briefs the TL or team.

Bodyguard

1. Originally (from the year 1735), "escort" or "those who serve a person of high position or rank."
2. In broad usage, an executive protection specialist or CPO.
3. On my details, we say "the Bodyguard" to refer to the CPO who stays with the protectee at all times and serves as Team Lead.

Certified Protection Operator

1. An executive protection specialist trained and certified under International Executive Protection. **Certified Protection Operator** and **CPO** are terms I coined and registered with the U.S. Patent Office so that we can speak about our discipline without confusing anyone, even those who have bought into the "bodyguard myth." Everyone on my teams is a CPO and carries a badge, except possibly the driver, who needs only a chauffeur license unless he's wearing other hats on the detail.

Client

1. Several terms are used interchangeably to designate our protectee. We may say **client, principal, subject,** or **asset.** In some cases, only **asset** reflects accurately the subject of protection—a detail may be assigned to transport a gemstone or sensitive device, or protect a trade secret. **Client** is literally the one who pays us, yet the protectees may include followers of the client.

Detail

1. An executive protection assignment.
2. The team (or individual) on an assignment. The protectee may be considered part of the detail.
3. "To detail" means to assign someone to a particular role or task.

Dynamic bodyguarding

We're moving about, driving, getting in and out of vehicles, walking next to clients, opening the doors, clearing rooms, securing the area, doing an advance. We are doing a forward, having the forwards there.

Executive protection

1. An appropriate substitute for "bodyguarding" in the sense of "serving a person of high position or rank." Executive protection is a team activity.

Forward

A forward is somebody who is already there when we show up. When they get there before me, they will do an advance. When I get off the plane, my team is there and they take me. Same thing when I do things with a client, I am there ahead of them. Or if I'm with my client, my forward team is already there. So I don't have to go there and recreate what they've already done.

Handler

1.   Senior staff members for a high-profile client.

Hard target

1.   A security presence designed to intimidate and deter would-be ag- gressors.
2.   A client who has secured his safety through a high level of protective measures

High-profile

Attracting a lot of attention, especially media attention.

Low-profile

Attracting little attention.

Perimeter

The area you control.

Pre-frame

To prepare someone in advance as to what to expect.

Profile

1.   Degree of recognition.

2. How one is perceived.
3. To assess the threat potential of an individual or activity.
4. To take action based on a stereotype, as in "racial profiling."

Profiling

1. To assess the threat potential of an individual or activity.
2. To take action based on a stereotype, as in "racial profiling."

Risk analysis

A study of the available intelligence regarding a situation, from the standpoint of dangers and threats.

Site survey

A scout of the destination site; *advance*.

Soft target

1. A security presence that is unobtrusive.
2. A person who is exposed and vulnerable to security threats.

Stalker

A person who follows another continuously as a form of harassment, possibly with intent to harm.

Static security

We're standing in one spot, such as looking at a plaza.

Surveillance

Observation of another's movements. May involve stake-outs, cameras, and GPS devices.

Team Lead (TL)

The actual bodyguard, who makes the decisions and stays with the client.

Appendix II

Reading List

Many times in this book I have recommended that you read as much as you can get your hands on. The ideas in these books have helped me every step of the way, so I want to give you a short list of my 30 favorite books plus a DVD.

Think and Grow Rich by Napoleon Hill

The Richest Man in Babylon by George S. Clason

The E Myth: Why Most Businesses Don't Work and What to Do About It by Michael Gerber. (He has a whole series of books.)

Seven Habits of Highly Effective People by Steve Covey

The Millionaire Next Door: The Surprising Secrets of America's Wealthy by Thomas J. Stanley and William D. Danko

How to Become CEO: The Rules for Rising to the Top of Any Organization by Jeffrey J. Fox

One Simple Idea: Turn Your Dreams into a Licensing Goldmine While Letting Others Do the Work by Stephen Key

Trump: The Art of the Deal by Donald J. Trump and Tony Schwartz

Trump: Think Like a Billionaire: Everything You Need to Know About Success, Real Estate and Life by Donald Trump

Investing for Income: A Bond Mutual Fund Approach to High-Return, Low-risk Profits by Ralph G. Norton

A Millionaire's Notebook: How Ordinary People Can Achieve Extraordinary Success by Steven K. Scott

Lenny Bogdanos

Stop Sitting on Your Assets by Marian Snow

The Go-Getter: The Classic Story That Tells You How to Be One by Peter B. Kyne

Passion Profit & Power: Reprogram Your Subconscious Mind to Create the Relationships, Wealth and Well-Being That You Deserve by Marshall Sylver

To Sell is Human: The Surprising Truth About Moving Others by Daniel H. Pink

The Millionaire Mind by Thomas J. Stanley

The 8th Habit: From Effectiveness to Greatness by Stephen R. Covey

Working Knowledge: How Organizations Manage What They Know by Thomas H. Davenport and Laurence Prusak

Eight $teps to $even Figure$: The Investment Strategies of Everyday Millionaires and How You Can Become Wealthy Too by Charles B. Carlson, CFA

Get the Edge: Personal Journal by Anthony Robbins

Personal Power: The Most Successful Personal Achievement Program of All Time by Anthony Robbins

Power with People by James K. Van Fleet

How to Sell Yourself by Joe Girard

The One Minute $ales Person by Spencer Johnson, M.D.

Unlimited Power by Anthony Robbins

The Power of Innovative Thinking: Let New Ideas Lead You to Success by Jim Wheeler

You Can Retire While You're Still Young Enougto Enjoy It by Les Abromovitz

True Success: A New Philosophy on Excellence by Tom Morris, Ph.D.

Empires of the Mind: Lessons to Lead and Succeed in a Knowledge-Based World by Denis Waitley

First Things First Every Day: Because Where You're Headed Is More Important Than How Fast You're Going by Stephen R. Covey

Small Business Success: The 7 Point Plan for Growing Your Business by Michael E. Gerber (DVD)

Appendix III

Eastman Success Story

My name is Brent Eastman. I was born in a small remote village of Castara in the twin island state of the Republic of Trinidad and Tobago. I am the eldest of three children and grew up in a large, extended, close-knit family with aunts, uncles, grandparents and plenty of cousins, where strong morals and spiritual values were practiced, and formative learning was encouraged in my household. I had an opportunity to attend secondary school where I obtained two subjects in the Caribbean examination council (CXC). Being in school was a bit challenging as my approach, thinking and mindset was somewhat different. I decide to focus on different avenues with the use of my knowledge in order to acquire a good living.

My drive for work started at the age of eighteen years, when I got a job as a security officer; there I was able to interact with people from different walks of life in society. I then moved into the health care environment in the departments of psychology and coroner. From there I elevated into the medical field by studying and becoming an Emergency Medical Technician.

My passion for the military started at a young age when I was a cadet in school, and while having conversations with my grandfather who served in World War II as a soldier. This inspired me to join the Defense Force Reserves, where I was successful in recruit training. I am currently serving in various fields as military investigator, military instructor and medic. During my time serving I was able to conduct community work by training civilians with various displays in march pass for sports and family days where soyme well executed routines were performed.

Lenny Bogdanos

The man who inspired me to join the military: Josey Eastman, my grandfather

My first opportunity to function as an operator outside of military duties was when an international artist visited Tobago and I was assigned as part of the security detail. Due to my professionalism the international operator engaged me in a conversation, explaining the professional approach to personal protection and international certification that will allow me to become more marketable in the executive protection industry. With this information, my curiosity arose, and I started doing research seeking more information about executive protection.

In researching International Executive Protection (IEP), I looked at the reviews that were written and the type of clients they engaged. This gave me the motivation to do the course with International Executive Protection (IEP).

The Level One training course in EP further cemented my initial interest from my research. The course structure, camaraderie, and the presentations were simple but effective; the information as it was disseminated made learning and understanding easy. This introduced me to the correct and professional approach to personal protection, which further motivated me to register immediately for Level Two. The instructors were very professional in executing their specific field, making sure all the students understood what was taught. The delivery was thorough and appropriate on all levels, and reviews were done on a regular basis throughout the sessions. Regardless of the students' backgrounds, everyone was able to learn and understand.

Level one class Tampa Florida

Level two class Tampa Florida

Out of the marketing skills and strategies that were learnt, my registered company was formed, and all the necessary professional structures learnt were applied. This is a limited liability company to allow for greater transparency in all its operations. This multifaceted company provides executive protection, executive transportation, complete background checks for employment purpose and private investigation. The logo was designed to facilitate specific identifications as to what EASTMAN'S EXECUTIVE PROTECTION SERVICES LTD denotes. No uniforms were designed. Instead, all of our operators would blend in with the occasion, ensuring that they are professionally and appropriately attired for any event. Operators should not be obvious.

A seal was designed for security purposes where any documents leaving the company will have its seal, stamp and signature to show authenticity. Call cards were made to allow for continuous contact or reference by clients. An office space was set up for business transactions to be organized professionally so that clients and employees can operate, creating greater privacy. The located area of the office is well secured with high-tech cameras situated inside and outside.

Company's logo and trademark

Ongoing efforts are being made to ensure that all employees are professionally trained by IEP and have credible character. I initiated for the IEP to do two consecutive bodyguard trainings in Tobago. I was able to assist with training personnel from different parts of the world with unique background in Tampa, Florida with IEP. This is in an effort to raise and maintain the standard of executive protection in Tobago and by extension Trinidad and the Caribbean so that they can operate with international standards.

First executive protection course in Tobago

Second executive protection course in Tobago

Assisting with training in Tampa, Florida

Executive Protection Service was instrumental in allowing me to venture into the world of work by providing executive protection for one of the most humble international artists, American singer-songwriter Ashanti, during one of Tobago's most popular event, the Great Fete concert, as well as regional artists during its jazz festival, We also had the privilege to provide executive protection for Dr. Wendelle Wallace, a university lecturer at the University of the West Indies Trinidad and Tobago campus at a National Gang Crime Research award function in Chicago, Illinois. It also gave me the confidence to experiment with the social media and network through these mediums. The ability to navigate through the internet helped to communicate with tutors and trainers, enhance my business, contact clients, recruit employees and communicate information on a timely basis. It also helped with correspondence, documents, application forms sent to clients and potential clients.

*Executive protection for
Dr. Wendelle Wallace in Chicago, Illinois*

*Executive Transportation details with
the Government of Trinidad and Tobago*

Agent Eastman with Ashanti in Tobago Great Fete

Agent Gift with Ashanti   *Agent Duncan with Ashanti*

Regardless of the status of the client (local, regional or international), the price remains constant with the emphasis being placed on professionalism through delivery and maintaining a high standard as per international requirements.

When I initially trained with IEP, most of the drills were new to me and were very challenging, but because of repetitions and because the instructors allowed trainees to correct mistakes as they went along, these drills were understandable and easier as the training progressed. These drills included:

Gun Takeaway

Gun takeaway drills showed me different ways to disarm my assailants within close proximity of me, and a safe way of doing so.

Dynamic Shooting

The dynamic shooting at the level I class added value to what I learnt in the military. Level II drills were more advanced and challenging, in that my existing military skills and bounding drills are different to that of a bodyguard, where you bound backwards while protecting your client compared to the military where you bound forward when covering fire is being suppress. Levels of safety and control on the range were maintained at all times. In the classes we were able to do more dynamic shooting and training because of the standard of the range. The Navy Seals and Marine instructors were at a high level, maintaining the acronym: EDI (Explain Demonstrate Imitate).

Bodyguard "Myth"

Reading and understanding the book, *The Bodyguard Myth,* assisted in a holistic way to the real concept and approach to bodyguarding (size does not matter as the skills learnt are what is important).

Lenny Bogdanos

EEPS company structure

Eastman's Executive Protection Services Ltd. (EEPS) company structure is set with a foundation for long-term investment in bodyguarding; profits will not be realized immediately but will be on the long-term. This type of business is relatively new and not popular on the island.

Feasibility studies show that this type of business has a great chance of survival and profitability as this need will grow on the island because of the pending tourism thrust which will allow businessmen/women, both local, regional and international, to operate within these shores.

Lifetime membership with IEP is very important to EEPS'existence. It will:

1. Allow for continuous training.
2. Keep the company up-to-date with new techniques and technolo- gies so that international status is maintained.
3. Promote Trinidad and Tobago as a hub for the training of body- guards.
4. Foster a stronger alliance with international tutors and trainers.
5. Introduce potential trainees and clients to IEP.
6. Have the ability to share local, regional and international experi- ences to enhance training manuals.

Fostering the relationship with our international brothers

QUOTE:

"To those who are looking to venture in this industry, do not stand by my side and look at the horizon I have created and am currently looking at; instead, stand on my shoulders and look beyond, creating your own and new horizon." Brent Eastman.

In conclusion, the IEP instructors left an impression that fueled an upward thrust and passion to bring this type of training to the Caribbean region, making the region a hub for bodyguard training which will allows individuals from far and beyond to experience and explore this training. The region has natural pollution-free terrain for outdoor training, which is conducive for a state-of-the-art range to be opened in this region. In the future I will like to provide this service throughout Trinidad and Tobago and the Caribbean region. Eastman's Executive Protection Service is expanding to create more employment and to be known as a premier international company with great successes and profits.

Appendix IV

Fluonia Success Story

My name is Deonarine Fluonia. I have been a Diplomatic Security Agent at Delta One Executive Protection Services since July, 2000. You can find me on Facebook as Diploguard and on LinkedIn.

Lenny Bogdanos

My career started as a Dutch Marine (Koninklijke Marine Amsterdam Infantry '88/'89-2). Using this as my foundation, I have cultivated executive protection skills, with the desire to continue increasing my skills to a very high level, and to learn world-class techniques.

My experience with International Executive Protection (IEP) has been important in achieving these goals, and I have taken full advantage of their systems of training and certifications.

Their courses include written materials and hands-on experience. The Level I course is a good preparation on the basic standard operating procedures and formations in the executive protection world. Level II is a much more advanced class and includes transitions from short guns to long guns and visa versa, with more movement and more dynamic target shooting.

Gun takeaway, taught in both Level I and Level II, is clearly demonstrated, clearly explained, and good hands-on experience. The dynamic shooting course, also taught in both levels, allows a student to develop perfect skills. A strong point throughout the courses taught are the cautions against the various bad habits that can cost you your life.

IEP instructors are very educated, motivated and inspiring. They are professional, sharp and always on point. Instructors request feedback, as the course is being taught, from the participants to get an accurate sense of how well students understand the subject. The IEP approach is to never leave a student behind. Students come away from an IEP course with the understanding that executive protection is more than just a job: it is a lifestyle.

As I trained with IEP, I gained a certainty that IEP would continue to help me grow within my field of expertise, and that is exactly what has happened. With IEP training, I learned business concepts that I have used to strengthen my executive protection agency and help make it successful, including how to successfully market myself. I have created a brand for myself, with logos, pens, social media, and literature and clothing. I have learned to use social media in a positive, healthy way.

In addition to strengthening my executive protection business with IEP training, I have become an IEP-affiliated instructor as well and have my own school in Aruba in addition to my security business. Instructors, day-to-day, receive continuing challenges in the line of duty. We are then able to exchange and share our professional skills.

The lifetime membership with IEP is important to me. This way we are able to keep up with any new international standards in executive protection training. Every year, my company brings 10 members to IEP for the advanced refreshment course. We also bring Lenny Bogdanos, founder of IEP, to the islands as a guest instructor to give my students a better understanding of the international executive protection world and bring that international connection to my students. I am certainly proud to refer others to train with IEP.

Every decision I have made has always been about mission success, what's best for the team. That's it, don't ever doubt that. *The Bodyguard Myth*, a book by IEP founder Mr. Bogdanos, and which is part of the IEP training, speaks of this ethic; I found that we speak the same language.

My Delta 1 Executive Protection Services provides highly trained and experienced armed and unarmed security officers and security teams. We can perform patrols utilizing foot, bicycles, ATVs, marked or unmarked vehicles. We provide a single point of contact, and the ability for consolidated invoicing for all locations. Our customized security solutions include providing officers in uniform or plain clothes, 24 hours a day, 7 days a week. Our security personnel can be in a number of uniform styles.

We achieve the highest level of quality control by utilizing effective screening and hiring policies, executed through regular training and testing. All D1 personnel are given thorough background checks, drug testing, and must meet current state requirements for training and licensing. We provide ongoing training programs for all levels of staff, tailored to the various locations of the details. Training courses include classroom instruction on general orders and site-specific post orders, operational and emergency procedures, use of security equipment, defensive tactics and interpersonal skills.

Lenny Bogdanos

Delta 1 management is available to our clients 24 hours a day, 7 days a week and can be contacted at diploguard@gmail.com. Supervisors make scheduled and unscheduled visits to ensure that our staff provides the highest level of service available in the industry.

Printed in the United States
By Bookmasters